Wedding Planner

A Guide to the Perfect Wedding

Brownlow Publishing Company
Fort Worth, Texas

Our

Wedding Planner

A Guide to the Perfect Wedding

Copyright © 1990
Brownlow Publishing Company, Inc.
6309 Airport Freeway / Fort Worth, Texas 76117

ISBN: 1-877719-09-9

Our Wedding Planner

The Wedding of

_____

and

_____

On

_____

Contents

Ten Steps to Your Perfect Wedding

See page 6 for complete list

Planning Guides

Introduction

*O*ne of the most marvelous things about planning your wedding is the opportunity to make a personal statement. Traditionally, the wedding is the bride's (oh, the groom's too, but the bride's in a special way), a gala celebration to be remembered for the rest of her life. The locations of the wedding and parties, the carefully chosen participants, your vows, the style and colors of the wedding attire, the decorations, the food — all of this paints your personal creation.

*M*ake that creation a masterpiece. This little book is just the place to get organized and take charge of your wedding with confidence. Whether you plan a large celebration or an intimate ceremony, formal or informal, traditional or utterly unique, make every moment a memory to be cherished.

CHAPTER ONE

Engagement

*C*ongratulations! The perfect beginning to the rest of your married lives was your engagement. However romantically, hilariously or practically your engagement was proposed and accepted, treasure that happy date in your memory. Perhaps you have a dried rose or some other memento. Has your fiancé written letters to you? If he has, tie them with a beautiful ribbon and put them away in a special place. If you do not already have a diary, you may want to begin one with the date of your engagement. Now is the time to initiate a photo album. Record meaningful experiences with photography, taking care to identify names, places and dates.

First Things First

Even now, protocol dictates that the first people to tell when you become engaged are your parents. A popular way to make the announcement is to invite each set of parents to separate, informal brunches, luncheons or dinners. If you prefer not to prepare the menu and create the restaurant with a table or booth that offers some privacy.

Introducing parents to parents is another propri-etary, common sense gesture of newly engaged couples. If the parents live near one another, you may arrange a small luncheon for them to express their welcome to the prospective son-in-law and daughter-in-law. Or if sched-ules or long distances hinder in-person introductions, either family may phone or write the other family to begin a friendship before the wedding. Giving special attention to family feelings will go a long way toward ensuring that your wedding celebration will be a festive occasion for all concerned.

Public Engagement Announcement

Phone your local newspaper, asking for the lifestyles editor, for the specific engagement announcement requirements — fees, deadlines, length of copy, photos. If you would like to include a photograph, you will probably need to send the editor a black-and-white glossy with your typewritten announcement. An appropriate formal engagement announcement is worded this way: "Mr. and Mrs. John Alexander of Plymouth Drive announce the engagement of their daughter, Elizabeth May, to Blake Harrison, the son of Mr. and Mrs. Sherwood Harrison of Philadelphia, Pennsylvania."

If your parents are divorced, a basic rule of etiquette would encourage the parent with whom you lived to make the announcement for you. Divorced parents may, however, agree to announce the engagement jointly, like this: "Mr. Ronald Erickson and Mrs. Jean Wilson…". If one of your parents is deceased, refer to that parent in the announcement as the "late Mr. (or Mrs.) Harrison." If your fiancé's family live in another area, place the announcement in their local newspaper as well.

You do not need to include a wedding date with your announcement. Plans for your wedding may take as long as two years or as little as two weeks, but you need not feel pressured into setting a date right away. However, you may already have set a wedding date. If you have, it is perfectly appropriate to include "A (specific date, a month or a season) wedding is planned" in your engagement announcement. You may wish to include biographical information as well, such as your and your fiancé's occupations, places of employment and location of your planned future home together. Be aware that some urban newspapers will print either your engagement announcement or your wedding announcement, but not both. Ask the newspaper editor about that if you are concerned.

Rings

The diamond ring and simple gold band are traditional engagement symbols, but not everyone opts for them. Traditionally, the fiancé selects, purchases and presents the ring to his bride-to-be. Now, both fiancé and fiancée very often agree on a budget, then select the ring together. Perhaps you could split the ring's expense, but you may rather let your fiancé pay for the ring and put some of your own finances in savings or investments that will benefit you both in a few years.

There are many styles of rings. Whatever you do, be sure to comparison shop. Look for the best quality for the best price within your budget. The more you study the market, the more likely you will be satisfied with your final choice.

You may choose a striking diamond solitaire or a half-carat diamond surrounded by smaller diamond baguettes. But there is no rule that states you must have a diamond. You may prefer a sapphire or perhaps an artistically, custom-designed gold band without a stone. Your engagement ring may be constructed to complement the wedding ring, entwining in a design incomplete without the wedding ring.

You and your fiancé may decide to purchase matching wedding rings. Otherwise, the groom's ring is usually a simple gold band, or a band with low, inset diamonds. Some men decline to wear rings, due to inconvenience. Although the symbol of the groom's wedding band is a beautiful one, there is no sense in imploring your fiancé to wear a ring against his wishes. Traditionally, the bride-to-be pays for the groom's ring; but again, traditions often bend to fit today's preferences and practicality.

Setting the Date

Schedules sometimes take priority over dreams and themes for wedding itineraries. What is your dream season of the year for your wedding? Is it spring with May lilacs and apple blossoms? What is your dream theme for a wedding? Is it Austrian (ethnic) with edelweiss flowers? Whatever your dreams, they require plans and commitments in advance. You need to consider:

✤ When would be the best time for you to schedule your wedding, honeymoon and preparation days as far as your occupations are concerned.

✤ When the site of your wedding and reception will be available, such as the church chapel, wildflower garden, oriental garden, or a friend's beautifully landscaped backyard.

✤ When your family and friends will be available, keeping in mind their vacation plans and business responsibilities, other weddings, anniversaries, babies' due dates, school and board examinations, and graduations.

Bride and Groom's Itinerary: An Overview

June, August, September, October and December are very popular wedding months. If you plan to be married then, you may need to allow yourself at least six months to make all of your arrangements. How much time you need to create your perfect wedding will depend on your preferences, sometimes the whims of the weather, and a host of other possibilities and downright surprises. So, as soon as you can,

✤ Decide on the wedding date, time and place; how many guests (and who); and what you plan to serve at your reception.

❧ *Bride:* Personally invite those whom you would like to participate as maid (unmarried) or matron (married) of honor, bridesmaids, flower girls, and ring bearer.

❧ *Groom*: Decide who will be best man, groomsmen and ushers.

❧ *Bride or groom:* Call the county government office to get information on requirements for a marriage license. If necessary, schedule physical examinations with your family doctor for blood tests.

❧ Never forget the all-important budget.

❧ Visit with your minister for his counsel and to make ceremony preparations.

❧ Hire a wedding consultant if you like, but do not be intimidated by his or her professionalism. This is your wedding, and it should reflect your dreams and wishes as well as your budget.

❧ Select and hire a professional caterer or request family friends to bake the wedding cake, prepare the food and serve it at your reception.

❧ Carefully select and hire a photographer. You may decide to have formal wedding portraits taken before the wedding.

❧ Choose musicians who will appear on time and perform without a hitch. Go over the music and ceremony program with them until you are sure that the harmony of sound will make your wedding ceremony ultra-special.

❧ Select and hire a florist who you know, preferably someone who will be able to deliver the out-of-season and difficult-to-find (and keep fresh) floral decorations when you need them and in excellent condition. Decide whether the florist will decorate the marriage and reception sites, whether your closest girlfriend would love to do the decorating (and do it well), or if you would like to do the decorating yourself to save money and meet your own standard of perfection. Be certain that the decorations will be done and in place just when needed. It is a good idea to find out when you can begin decorating. What time will the church and the reception hall be open so that decorations can be put into place? Is there a wedding right before or after yours that could complicate preparations?

❧ Choose your wedding theme and style, colors, bridal and attendants' gowns, groom and groomsmen's attire. *Bride*: Let your mother and mother-in-law know the colors you have chosen so they can order their wedding dresses to complement your style and color selections. While the attendants are on your mind, think about thank-you gifts for them and then purchase them whenever you have the time.

❧ *Groom*: Buy thank-you gifts for your best man, groomsmen and ushers.

❧ *Groom:* Ask someone you trust to register and watch over wedding gifts at your reception.

❧ *Bride:* If your fiancé hasn't already given you an engagement ring and selected a wedding ring, order those heirloom items as a couple. *Groom*: Keep the rings in a safe place and be sure they are at the church on time.

❧ Discuss changing your wills, life insurance and health insurance policies.

❧ Register your preferences for china, silver, glassware, linens, appliances and other household items at one or two local department stores.

❧ Discuss honeymoon plans with travel agents if

necessary. Confirm reservations, pick up tickets and purchase traveler's checks.

🙠 *Bride:* Organize your trousseau and travel kit. If possible, designate one closet as your trousseau closet. Pack needed travel items and whatever attire that can be folded in suitcases. The more you do ahead of time the easier it will be for you to "relax" as the time of your wedding approaches. *Groom*: Your wardrobe may be simpler than your bride's, but be sure you have everything ready for your honeymoon.

🙠 Order wedding invitations (engraved stationery may require six weeks).

🙠 *Bride:* Send wedding invitations with a deadline for response. Hopefully you will have already discussed key participants' personal schedules and know they will be able to attend the wedding, so reserve rooms for attendants and guests from out-of-town. The day after the invitation response deadline, reserve rooms for other out-of-town guests who request them.

🙠 *Bride:* Order thank-you notes.

🙠 *Bride:* Make hair appointments. You may want your hair cut a week or two before the wedding, if you're afraid it may be cut too short.

🙠 Look over your new home together and move as much furniture and household items into it as you can before the wedding. A comfortably furnished dwelling will be an attractive relief on your return from your honeymoon.

🙠 Whatever you do, keep all wedding participants posted as to dates, times and responsibilities.

The last week before your wedding could be especially hectic, if fun. Bride, you may give or attend a bridesmaids' party, during which you may present the thank-you presents to your bridesmaids; and groom, you may give or go to a bachelor's party. You will present your thank-you gifts to the best man, groomsmen and ushers at the rehearsal dinner. The rehearsal should be run through as smoothly as possible.

Take care of yourselves. Although you have your regular occupations and routines with which to contend, you now have all of the adjustments, obligations, joys, romance, enchantment and stress that come with a new life together.

NOTE: If this seems like a lot to do, don't panic. Start out by reserving the things that are most important to you. For example, if the church and the photographer are the most important elements, set your wedding date around their schedules and proceed from there. Remember, at first all you need to do is reserve your suppliers — details can be worked out later when you've had more time to think things through.

CHAPTER TWO

Meeting With the Minister

*Y*ou have three reasons to meet with your minister: (1)for premarital counseling, (2)to structure and personalize your wedding ceremony, and (3)to ask questions about chapel or sanctuary, reception hall and kitchen facilities; available vocalists and instrumentalists; suggestions for ceremony music; a changing room for the bride and her bridesmaids; handicap access and facilities; honorariums or fees; your marriage license, etc.

For Better, Not for Worse

The minister's goal (and yours) for your marriage is a home partnership in which Christ-centered love, mutual respect and permanent fulfillment will stand against all the disappointments and discouraging influences of your future together. He will gently remind you that marriage is a divine institution, created and blessed by God — far more than a civil, economic or social arrangement.

mutual, voluntary consent. The union is designed to be exclusive and lifelong. For spiritual oneness and marital harmony, both partners need to be consecrated to the Lord Jesus Christ and His will for their lives. Christ is the Lord of the home, the husband is His appointed leader, and the wife is His appointed helper. Loving self-sacrifice and generosity are hallmarks of His presence and essential elements of happiness. Finally, "Whatsoever ye do in word or deed, do all in the name of the Lord Jesus" (Colossians 3:17, KJV).

The amount of time the minister spends with you in premarital counseling will depend upon your ages, spiritual maturity and desire to use his marriage counseling experience and Biblically founded wisdom in the development of a happy Christian marriage and family. If you have questions about your (or your future partner's) understanding of God's grace and the importance of faith, the power of prayer, the holiness of Christian courtship and marriage (sex as God created it, the importance of purity and fidelity, the family as He blessed it), family devotions and spiritual growth, this is the time to ask them.

Marriage License

Although a marriage license can be purchased for a relatively insignificant sum and civil authorities can pronounce two people husband and wife within a matter of minutes, a Christian marriage is more than obedience to a civil ordinance. The cost of a marriage is more than any amount of money can cover; the actual cost is a lifetime commitment. Wherever the wedding is performed, informally on a sandy Hawaiian beach or formally in a church, God's presence should always be reverentially acknowledged. Because He originally ordained the institution of marriage, He is the ultimate authority under which a marriage is established. The occasion demands at least a few words of Scripture, a short message by the minister, marriage vows, exchange of rings and a prayer for God's guidance. Some couples even include the signing of the marriage license in the wedding ceremony, emphasizing the contractual nature of their union.

When you meet with your minister, ask him where to obtain your marriage license (unless you already know), when to give it to him and how many witnesses are required at its signing. If you are interested in including the signing in your wedding ceremony, ask him how it might be appropriately incorporated.

Wedding Ceremony

A basic program includes:
- the prelude;
- the first and second solos;
- the processional;
- welcome;
- giving the bride away,
- prayers, readings, choir selection or third solo;
- exchange of vows;
- presentation of ring, or exchange of rings;
- pronouncement of marriage;
- benediction and blessing;

✻ recessional; and
✻ postlude.

Suggestions for Customizing Your Ceremony

WELCOME GUESTS UPON THEIR ARRIVAL

Have attendants or ushers hand guests candles, decorated rice bags or flowers.

THE PROCESSIONAL

While the Bride's father traditionally escorts her down the aisle, it may be more practical for you to have your groom escort you. Stop to kiss your mothers, who are seated in the front pews, and give each of them a flower.

WELCOME

Ask your minister to not only welcome your guests on this very special occasion, but also create an atmosphere for worship. You may never see some of these people again, and many may have come long distances. Your wedding service is your opportunity to share your faith in Jesus Christ, the greatest gift you could ever give them in return for the honor of their presence.

GIVING THE BRIDE AWAY

Adaptations in this symbolic ritual are becoming

more common. The minister, who would customarily say, "Who gives this woman in marriage?" (addressing your father), might now say, "Who blesses this marriage?" (addressing both families, which respond with a resounding, "We do."). An addition to the ritual would be the Unity Candle ceremony, in which both families are requested to come and stand with you and your groom in front of three candles. Each family lights one of the candles, reserving the center candle for the two of you to light at the end of the ceremony.

Prayers, Readings, Choirs (vocal and handbell), Solos and Instrumentals

Your choices may range as wide as your imagination and budget permits, but remember the seriousness of the occasion as well as the joy. Popular music selections include "First Organ Sonata," by Mendelssohn; "Jesu, Joy of Man's Desiring," by Bach; "Ave Maria," by Schubert; "Hallelujah Chorus" from The Messiah, by Handel; "One Hand, One Heart" from West Side Story, by Bernstein and Sondheim; and "Ode to Joy," by Beethoven. Depending upon the theme or style of your wedding, you may choose inspirational soul (such as "We Are Not Ashamed," by Andraé Crouch), country gospel (such as "If That Isn't Love," by Dottie Rambo), a favorite old hymn (such as "O Perfect Love," "Happy the Home When God Is There" or "The Lord's Prayer") or popular gospel (such as "The Family of God," by William and Gloria Gaither, or "The Bond of Love," by Otis Skillings).

Customary music selections for the processional

and recessional include "Bridal Chorus" from Lohengrin ("Here Comes the Bride"), by Wagner; "Trumpet Voluntary," by Clark; and "Wedding March" from A Midsummer Night's Dream, by Mendelssohn. Again, you may prefer something different. A suggestion for the recessional might be "Theme from Chariots of Fire," by Vangelis.

EXCHANGE OF VOWS

Perhaps the constant use of the simple, traditional vows is reason enough for the growing number of custom-made vows. Somehow, rewording the service or memorizing the vows or reading letters of commitment reflects a determination to live up to them. The whole program, from start to finish, should suit both bride and groom from the viewpoints of good taste and their personal abilities to speak or sing in the public spotlight. If you plan to memorize and say your vows (not just repeating after the minister), it would be wise for the minister to have a copy of the vows ready at hand.

If you do choose to personalize your vows (there are no legal requirements, but your minister should approve them before the ceremony), study the traditional vows first. Thoroughly understand their meaning, and then consider what the marriage covenant means to you. You may decide to retain all of the traditional material or modify it according to your personal convictions and beliefs, adding some quotations from the Song of Songs (Song of Solomon). Vows should take no longer than three minutes. Your thoughts about marriage (for example, your faith, your goals, etc.) may be expressed in other ways during the marriage program, such as through music or poetry recitations.

This time spent with the minister will be helpful to both of you. His experience and guidance will pay rich dividends in the days of preparation for marriage and in the years of married life to come.

CHAPTER THREE

Pre-Wedding Parties

Engagement Party

Once you and your fiancé have informed both sets of parents of your momentous decision to marry, practically everyone you know will soon share the news. If your (the bride's) parents take the initiative to organize a party immediately, your father may have a very real chance of announcing the news to people who have not already heard it. Of course, your friends may have suspected the inevitability of your marriage since they have been following your courtship rather closely. In that event, your father may candidly make invitations for an official engagement party. Gifts, by the way, are not expected at an engagement party; but then, you need not offend anyone by not accepting a gift. It would be an appropriate gesture on your part to thank your engagement-party hosts, whether your parents or your in-laws, with a note and token of your appreciation.

No rule dictates that your parents are bound by social obligation to host an engagement party, nor is your honor. Friends at work may celebrate with you during lunch hour at a downtown restaurant. Sisters and brothers may toast you and your prospective husband at a special get-together. There is one rule that must be adhered to, however. Only people who will be invited to your wedding should be invited to your engagement parties.

Planning Party

Are you overwhelmed by questions (your own and others'), working out a budget without knowing how much money you will really need to spend, compiling guest lists, trying to find the perfect site for your wedding, phoning hotels and motels to compare their prices and facilities, checking on wedding styles and themes, engraved invitations, thinking about parties and thank-you gifts? What is wrong with a little "Help!"

Your goal is to have an affordable wedding, but also the perfect wedding...the wedding of your dreams. Unless you prefer to have a professional wedding consultant, you may discover to your delight that most women love weddings. Your close friends will help; they have a special interest in this wedding — you. Your relatives (including future in-laws) who live nearby will be excited about the prospect of your wedding; solicit their help, too. Especially consider the very special people who will be your maid of honor and attendants. Let them share in what can be the best time of your life — making this the most meaningful, wonderful, sentimental, romantic wedding ever created. Use the guide sheet titled "Getting It Together" for this party.

Who can bake the wedding cake? Who can organize the food preparations for the reception? Pour coffee? Replenish, or freshen, the serving trays? Who would like to greet guests as they arrive for the wedding ceremony? Register the gifts? Who can oversee the bridesmaids' dressmaking or alterations? Who could hardly wait to shop for that wedding gown with the "Exclusively Yours" on the label?

Who is great at floral arrangements and interior decorating? Who can sing, recite poetry, play an instrument? Who could design a polished wedding invitation, have it typeset and engraved on beautiful wedding stationery, and all at a reasonable dollar figure?

Do you know what will make every bit of assistance worthwhile to these people? Your honest and open appreciation...your happy smile and enthusiasm...your, thank-you notes and small gifts. A thoughtfully prepared luncheon or simply cake and punch can kick off an effective working party. Enjoy the teamwork and very important duties (not one part of the wedding preparation can be considered unimportant). And think about this: simplicity of design, tried-and-tested methods, and ingenuity will save hours of hard work.

Bridal Shower

Bridal showers traditionally have been hosted by close friends and not mother or mother-in-law, and have been an all female gathering. Now, "co-ed" showers are becoming popular. Because couples attend together, showers are often given after work hours or on weekends. Styles vary, from Sunday brunches to evening dessert parties.

Bridal shower gifts, especially at all-women parties, are customarily personal items (lingerie, wedding travel kit items, sachets, perfumes, etc.). A young bride may appreciate gifts designed to stock her new home (appliances, rugs, linens, kitchen·utensils, etc.). A more mature bride, particularly one who has all her household goods may appreciate gifts geared to her special interests (e.g., a china teapot, Hummel figurines, crystal bells, a perennials garden [gladiolus, tulip or iris bulbs may be welcome additions], thimbles, antique dolls, pressed wildflower designs, etc.).

As the honored guest, you may or may not be asked for suggestions or preferences; but you can be prepared with a well-thought-out response.

Bridesmaids' Party

Your bridesmaids are your special friends. You may have known them for "umpteen" years, and they know you very well. Out of their love for you, they've participated in one of the biggest events of your life — your wedding. Now it is your turn to reciprocate. What can you do?

Thank them with a private luncheon during the afternoon before your evening wedding (or a few days earlier to avoid stress). You know what your friends like.

Prepare them a gourmet meal at your place. Use your best linen. Decorate with fresh-cut flowers. When they arrive, welcome each one as the dear friend she is. Perhaps a professional caterer or maid could prepare the meal, serve it and then put things away so that you and your attendants can enjoy yourselves. A couple of hours of reminiscing and thinking about the future's bright hopes will refresh all of you.

Bachelors' Party

Sometimes, a "co-ed" party may appeal to all of you. Or, the groom may opt for the traditional male-friends get-together, adapting it to a special interest (e.g., a football game or a formal dinner at a special restaurant). This offers the bridegroom an opportunity to present thank-you gifts to his best man and groomsmen. If it would be more convenient, the bride and groom could present their thank-you gifts at the rehearsal dinner.

Rehearsal Dinner

An evening Rehearsal Dinner customarily precedes or follows the wedding-ceremony rehearsal. Because the dinner is scheduled the night before the wedding, it has the potential of being a happy occasion for all of the wedding participants, including you and your groom. Whereas most of the wedding preparations and costs have leaned on the shoulders of the bride and her family (unless other arrangements have been made), the Rehearsal Dinner is traditionally the contribution of the groom and his family.

The dinner may be formal or informal, buffet-style or sit-down. Often it is held in a private room at a hotel or club. Ideally, the wedding participants would have no responsibilities other than to enjoy themselves and help to make everyone feel welcome. If you and your groom have not already presented thank-you gifts to your attendants and groomsmen, this is an appropriate time.

NOTE: Some couples use the dinner following the rehearsal as a celebration that includes not only the wedding party, but out-of-town family and special guests. This gives the Bride and Groom a little more time to visit with special people who have traveled long distances to wish them well.

CHAPTER FOUR

Smart Buying on a Budget

 an you have a beautiful wedding on a budget? Yes, you can if you study the wedding market, construct a reasonable budget and develop a sound strategy to create the wedding of your dreams.

Basic Wedding Costs

The following list should start you thinking about your wedding costs. You may use only some of the items listed or all and more. Go through the bride's magazines for traditional and contemporary wedding ideas, check out the wedding shops, talk with your maid or matron of honor and attendants. Get all of the information you need so that you can organize your list of wedding items. You can expect to budget for all except what you can borrow; and you should think about sending thank-you notes and gift tokens of appreciation for what you borrow, too.

๛ Who traditionally pays for what? Who will for your wedding? What is the bride responsible for? What is the groom responsible for?

ʕ Wedding and reception site (church or park facilities rental, reception hall rental).

ʕ Invitations, thank-you notes and postage. Will there be a calligrapher's fee? Will the invitations be engraved or thermographed [similar in appearance but less expensive).

ʕ Wedding and honeymoon attire (wedding gown, headpiece and shoes; bridesmaids' gowns [handmade, ordered from a catalog or custom-made] and shoes; groomsmen's tuxedos and shoes [rented]; mothers' gowns and shoes; flower girl's dress and shoes, ring bearer's tuxedo and shoes, honeymoon wardrobe, clothing alterations).

ʕ Flowers, candles and ribbons, as well as staples, glue, straight pins and whatever other little items are necessary (engagement party bouquets and centerpieces, bridesmaids' party and groomsmen's party bouquets and centerpieces, rehearsal dinner bouquets and centerpieces, wedding chapel candles and bouquets [including beribboned nosegays and candles on the inside of the aisle side pews, and candles at the front of the chapel [which the ushers light before the ceremony, or the three candles used in the Unity Ceremony mentioned on page 22], tent decorations [if the wedding is held outdoors], bride's and bridesmaids' nosegays, mothers' corsages, groom's and groomsmen's boutonnieres, fathers' boutonnieres, reception buffet and table centerpieces).

ʕ Ceremony fees and honorariums (minister's fee, musicians' fees or honorariums).

ʕ Food and beverages (parties and reception, including wedding cake).

ʕ Photography (formal engagement and bridal portraits, traditional wedding photographs, candid wedding shots [which could be taken by friends], videotaping, albums and extra prints for family and friends).

- Ring(s).
- Thank-you gifts.
- Marriage license.
- Equipment rental (punch bowls, china and silver, linens, trays, tables and chairs, tent, special lighting, stereo and cassette disks, sound equipment and electrical hookup).
- Hairstyling and barbering.
- Bridesmaids' and groomsmen's accommodations, if needed.
- Honeymoon accommodations and travel expenses.
- Gratuities.

In an earlier age, most of the wedding expenses were expected to be paid by the bride's family and fiscal responsibility resided on her father's capable shoulders. Now that is not necessarily the case. Many couples split the wedding costs without waiting for their parents to offer contributions. In their twenties and thirties, moving up in their careers, many couples planning weddings today are financially on their own.

Whether Dad takes over, or you and your fiancé assume the entire obligation of wedding expenses, you need to provide the list of wedding requirements and corresponding costs. To track all of this information, use the guide sheets provided in the last half of this planner to simplify the budget process.

Total Costs

When you have an Estimated Grand Total of expenses, subtract that from your Budget Maximum. Either you will have to come up with more expense money or keep your expenses within the current Budget Maximum.

To trim costs, make whatever can be made (e.g., bride's and bridesmaids' gowns, garter, ring pillow, centerpieces and any flower arrangements, pew aisle decorations). Use flowers that are in season. At your reception, serve simple hors d'ouevres and cake rather than a formal meal. Have family or friends bake and decorate the wedding cake. For more ideas, see "Planning Party" on page 26. Inquire about group rates at motels; discounts are usually offered for blocks of rooms. Guests generally cover their own lodging and travel expenses.

You may find that a wedding consultant can save you money as well as time. Do some comparison shopping for wedding consultants to see what they offer and what they charge. Then compare that information with the figures you have already gathered. Wedding consultants receive special rates on supplies, so they could pass those savings on to you. Some even offer free services because they receive commissions from suppliers on purchases and rentals you make through them.

Above all, keep an accurate expense record. Sales tax, gratuities, cancellation fees and other possibly overlooked costs (e.g., blood tests, reception coat check, parking fees, microphone fee, dress alteration charges, power generator and lights for tent, maps to the ceremony and reception sites) may expand your budget.

CHAPTER FIVE

Flowers

*F*lowers are such an important part of the wedding celebration, a romantic statement of how special this day is for you and your fiancé. Unfortunately, it is also the area where you have the least control, since you cannot see your fresh arrangements until the morning of the wedding.

Choose Your Florist Early

To avoid disappointment, begin to look for a good florist as soon as the wedding date is set. You don't need to know the details of your wedding to decide who will be the best supplier. Check photographs of past weddings, ask questions to see how willing the suppliers are to accommodate your unique ideas and how knowledgeable they are about flowers (i.e., what will be in season, what flowers hold up best, etc.). Most importantly, get recommendations from friends and family. Once you have chosen the florist, the florist can reserve time on his calendar to service your wedding, and you can decide on the

Once it is time to plan each arrangement, provide your florist with as much information as possible. Give details of dress styles and swatches of fabric as well as a list of special people you'd like to honor with flowers. One note of caution: make sure that by giving flowers to one person, you don't unintentionally exclude another. You may decide it's best to express your appreciation in a more private manner to avoid hurt feelings.

It's also a good idea to visit the ceremony and reception sites with the florist to plan the decorations. You may decide to use a lot of bows with greenery to keep costs down. Or you may chose to do floral arrangements in silk if you can use them in your home after the wedding.

There are many ways to keep costs down; but once you begin planning details, it is important to record on the contract the number of blossoms and approximate sizes so that you and your florist share the same vision of what your wedding flowers will look like. The guide sheet on page 71 will help you to keep track of this important information.

CHAPTER SIX

Wedding Guest List and Invitations

our guest list may involve only intimate friends, family members and members of the wedding party; but deciding on the guest list is a primary step in planning your wedding. Until you know how many people are coming, you cannot make reasonable estimates for wedding invitations, facilities, wedding attire and a myriad of crucial details.

Number of Guests

Of course, you may arrive at the number of people from different perspectives: budget, your preferences and the facilities of your choice. Your fiancé will provide you with a list of names, too — all of them from among his family and friends. How many and who will attend are two issues that you should agree upon. You could decide on a total number, then allot half for your family and friends and half for his. Or, you could allot a third of the number

GATHER ADDRESSES AND PHONE NUMBERS

The engagement party is the ideal place to gather names and addresses of prospective wedding guests. Ideally, parents of both families will be present. In that event, phone your mother and future mother-in-law ahead of time, requesting them to bring their address books to the party. If friends are invited too, you can ask them for their addresses and phone numbers there (if you do not have that information).

"MAKE ROOM" WITH A POST-WEDDING PARTY

You and your fiancé may have large families, a great many friends, or family and friends in another part of the country. Think about scheduling a second reception or informal post-wedding party for them (a week or two weeks after your honeymoon). For those who you think would like to attend this party, insert a typewritten (and signed) or matching invitation card inside the formal wedding invitation. Include a date deadline for guests to respond, letting you know how many and who will attend. Most people would prefer to attend either the formal wedding reception or the post-wedding party; only a few very close friends would attend both, particularly if long distances are involved. This "second reception" works especially well if one of your families lives out of town: many of their friends won't be able to travel to the wedding but would love to congratulate the new couple at a special reception closer to home. This would be the perfect time to show your wedding video — or you may want to wear your wedding gown again!

The Wedding Invitation

You will be addressing friends, family, co-workers, perhaps even neighbors, inviting them all to share in one of the momentous celebrations of your life — your wedding. You will have known many of these people since you were born. In addition, you know that they will go out of their way to make your wedding memorable because they love you. How will you approach them by written invitation?

The formal wedding invitation is traditionally engraved on folded white or ivory paper, sometimes parchment and sometimes with an embossed border. A small square of loose tissue paper protects the engraved type. The card and tissue are inserted into an envelope bearing the recipient's handwritten name, and this envelope is inserted into another envelope, which is hand-addressed and stamped. Many people include hotel information and maps of wedding and reception sites for out-of-town guests. This makes them feel like you really want them to attend.

FORMAL COPY VS. INFORMAL COPY

Your wedding invitation supplier can show you numerous examples of the formal, traditional wording. In recent years, a less formal, more personal style has also become acceptable.

INVITATIONS WELL WITHIN THE BUDGET

If monetary and time constraints are of concern to

you, several alternatives are available to you:

    🌢 Phone nearby family and friends, avoiding the cost of written invitations altogether;

    🌢 Handwrite your invitations on small, ready-made note cards;

    🌢 Prepare the entire invitation layout yourself with the help of a local "quick-printer;" or,

    🌢 Decrease the number of invitations to be sent out by inviting the members of your church through the church bulletin.

PHONE KEY GUESTS

Before sending any wedding and post-wedding-party invitations, phone key prospective guests. They will feel especially welcome and honored. Have motel and hotel information ready to give them over the phone; and if necessary, send them maps of hotel and motel locations, as well as of the wedding and reception sites.

KEEP TRACK OF INVITATION RESPONSES

Be sure to record responses as they arrive. Generally, you can predict that 2/3 of the guests who receive the wedding invitation will attend. You should be able to expect everyone who accepted the invitation to show up, and many a bride has wisely estimated more people to show up than were invited. If you are planning on a large, formal dinner at a country club, you would do well to retain some leeway.

CHAPTER SEVEN

Wedding Attire

ove for a lifetime is reflected in the wedding couple's desire to please each other, including their wedding attire. The graceful bride wears her finery in all good taste. Her groom's impeccable tailoring complements his quiet confidence. On this day, of all days, everything about the wedding couple and their party should honor God. On this day, two people are bonding themselves to each other and to His will in a permanent covenant.

Lovingly designed and sewn or heirloom attire — "something old, something new, something borrowed, something blue" — often symbolizes a stable, mature and continuing relationship. Purchased readymade or rented wedding costumes, suiting the mood and budget of a bride and groom, could do as well as any other. Under certain circumstances, informal yet elegant clothing may express a sophistication that no other style could provide.

The best way to begin your search for the perfect dress is to look through bridal magazines to narrow down the styles you are considering. You may want to take these pictures with you to the bridal salon to help you locate your dress more quickly. It's also helpful if you have a price range in mind — many dresses of similar style vary widely in price due to fabric or lace. Having a budget in mind will protect you from falling in love with a dress that is out of your reach.

Whatever styles, colors, fabrics, trims and accessories appeal to you will be appropriate for you. You have the ultimate say, so do not allow this season's fashions and commercial advertising to intimidate you. Be true to your own ideals, dreams and taste.

Basic Guidelines for Wedding Attire

The following simplified, popular categories should aid you in your quest for the most attractive and appropriate wedding attire. Which style suits you best? Formal, semi-formal, informal?

FORMAL

Bride: Floor-length dress with train; matching gloves and shoes; hat or hem- to fingertip-length veil; elaborate bouquet.

Groom: (Daytime) Black or gray stroller (walking coat), striped trousers, gray waistcoat, white shirt with turned-down collar, striped tie, black shoes and socks. (After six o'clock) Black or charcoal gray dinner jacket with matching trousers, white pleated-front shirt with turn-down collar, black vest or cummerbund, black shoes and socks, black bow tie.

SEMI-FORMAL

Bride: Floor-length dress with ankle-length veil or street-length dress with short veil, hat or flowers in hair; matching shoes; small bouquet.

Groom: Solid dark suit, white shirt, four-in-hand tie, black shoes and socks.

INFORMAL

Bride: Street-length suit or dress with nosegay, wristlet posy or corsage. (Hand-held nosegay, wristlet posy and pinned corsage are all little bunches of flowers, ribbons and beads.)

Groom: Suit and other accessories to harmonize stylistically with bride's attire.

Mothers customarily wear long dinner dresses for formal evening celebrations, in colors that blend with the bridesmaids' floor-length dresses. For semi-formal and informal celebrations, mothers would select street-length dresses similar to the bridesmaids', although harmonizing rather than matching.

Bridesmaids' and flower girl's attire is usually similar in style to the bride's, but modified to a certain extent and in color. Complementing every individual in the party is of the utmost importance, so make your selections carefully and emphasize the necessity of a perfect fit and precise tailoring.

The groom, fathers and groomsmen wear matching attire. It should be noted that formal and semi-formal men's wear is becoming far less formal, especially for daytime weddings. The traditional concept in the formal and semi-formal categories already mentioned, although not outmoded, is being employed less frequently in favor of contemporary formal suits (white or light colors for spring and summer, darker colors for fall and winter). The ring bearer customarily wears an Eton suit with short pants and knee socks. The older the ringer bearer, however, the more likely he will match the attire of the men in the wedding party.

CHAPTER EIGHT

Reception

ormal wedding ceremonies are usually followed by a formal reception with hors d'oeuvres followed by a sit-down dinner or buffet. Informal ceremonies, especially popular among more mature bridal couples and for second weddings, may suggest sophisticated sit-down dinners at exclusive clubs or luxury hotels. Other informal weddings may be concluded with a picnic in the park or an at-home reception with plasticware and paper plates.

Reception Site

What do you do? Ask the manager of each possible reception site these questions (you may think of more, depending upon your actual situation, requirements and preferences):

᠅ Do you have adequate facilities to manage a buffet for _____ people?

᠅ Do you have a private reception hall adequate to seat _____ people (allowing a margin of 18 for additions to the guest list)?

✎ Will that reception hall be available on (date) between (time-time)? What is the rental fee for six hours? Are there overtime charges? Are there any other people renting this spot that day that may inhibit decorating or rush our celebration?

✎ In the unlikely (but who knows the future?) event that we would have to cancel our reservation, would the deposit be refundable? What is the law regarding cancellation of a contract?

✎ Do you have adequate air conditioning (or heating, depending upon the season) to make the reception hall comfortable?

✎ Do you have a perfectly in-tune piano, microphones and sound equipment available? Are there rental charges for their use? Any extra electrical hookup charges? How are the acoustics in the reception hall? Is there any regulation regarding sound decibels?

✎ Do you recommend any musical groups?

✎ Could we hire our own musicians and use their microphones and sound equipment? Would there be a charge for the electrical hookup?

A note regarding the hiring of musicians: Know the musicians firsthand, their style, the quality of their performances. Beware the mere spoken word. Insist on a written, signed contract stating the name, instrument and role of each musician contracted to appear in person; the date and reception-site address, the time to begin playing and the time to stop (including overtime fee); the style of music or specific songs; and the musicians' kind of attire. This will protect against a talent company substituting other musicians under the same "group name". (e.g. three bands with the same name.)

⚘ Is there a comfortable lounge area outside of the reception hall where guests could sit down or walk around and mingle? Could that be cordoned off and reserved for our guests until we in the wedding party arrive from the photography session at the church? How much would you charge for that? Will their be people from other parties cutting through our reception area?

⚘ How much would you charge for butlered hors d'oeuvres and beverages in the lounge area?

⚘ May our florist decorate the reception hall and lounge area?

⚘ Where could we have the receiving line? The Guest Book?

The Guest Book should be placed on a pedestal where guests will see it immediately, either before they go through the receiving line or afterward. An attendant should stand or sit by the Guest Book and encourage guests to sign it. Sometime during the dinner, they could take it around the reception room to catch those who may have missed it.

⚘ Where should the gift table go?

A word to the wise: You may want to assign a close friend to monitor the wedding gifts. Preferably, guests would send the gifts to your home; but, no doubt, some guests will take gifts to the wedding ceremony and others to the reception. Gifts should not be opened at either the wedding or the reception. Some newlyweds invite a small group of friends and family to a brunch on the morning after the wedding, where they open their presents and guests have an opportunity to "ooh" and "ahh."

৯৯ Could you provide a raised platform for the head table?

৯৯ Do you have at least two large rooms where the wedding party could change into travel clothes after the reception?

৯৯ Do you have adequate, convenient parking? What type of parking facilities do you have? Would guests be charged for parking? Is valet parking a possibility?

৯৯ Are there any "rules of the house" that we need to know about (e.g., decorations, band size, coat check, security)?

৯৯ Are there any other charges (e.g., restroom, parking attendants, coat check, security)?

৯৯ Do you carry liability insurance?

৯৯ Do you have references from satisfied clients?

৯৯ Would you be willing to write up a contract, specifying every detail of the costs, and sign it if we decide to use these facilities?

৯৯ How much advance time do you need in order for us to confirm the reservation? What is your deadline for our final guest count?

৯৯ In what form do you expect payment? By check or credit card?

৯৯ When can someone come in to decorate and who is responsible for clean-up?

Now you can ask the manager about catering services.

Did you think the long list of questions was at last complete? You can see that finding out what you need to know can take some time. If you do not have the time, and you cannot assign someone whom you trust implicitly to manage this project, you may want to consider hiring a reception consultant to do the work for you. Of course, you or a friend must take some time to select a consultant who will meet your standards at your price. Do you know anyone who has used a consultant? Start there.

Catering and Cakes

💦 Do you have a catering specialist who would be available to serve the buffet for _____ people?

💦 What are the prices?

💦 Are there overtime fees?

💦 Is there a list of references?

💦 How many waiters would the buffet require? There should be one waiter to every ten people. Who serves the wedding cake?

💦 Could you recommend a baker you've worked with to do the wedding cake?

💦 Can they set up the cake on the day of the reception?

💦 Is there a set buffet menu, or could we make our own buffet selections?

💦 Would the costs you quote now change at all? Prices should not go up more than 10%, and they should be locked-in 90 days before the wedding.

💦 Could my fiancé and I taste samples from your buffet menu?

You may be surprised by the reception-site managers' initial quotes, but you will certainly be wiser for the information. Your original desires may have to be modified, perhaps not. When you're satisfied with facts and figures, obtain reservation confirmations and make sure firm, signed contracts are made.

Reception Photography

(Contracted photographer's package, friends' snapshots, professional and/or friends' videotaping)

When selecting a professional photographer, you need to:

- Look at sample photos closely.
- Decide when the photos will be taken —
  before or after the ceremony.
- Contract for the actual photographer —
  not his assistant.
- List photos and locations to be taken.
- List people in the photos
  (i.e. grandparents, etc.).

Professional photographers have been known to disappear before the cake cutting. Oh, yes. If a photographer has been hired for a certain number of hours (say three), he may not wait around to see if you are interested in paying an overtime fee. Please take that eventuality into consideration when you sign a contract for his services.

There is another thought. You may be grateful for those bright little bulbs having been popped off in your and your guests' faces during the reception. Friends' snapshots often capture memories like no "candids" taken by a professional photographer, and they make great backups in case of unforeseen disaster. Their flashes, however, can get in the way of the professional photographer's flash and spoil your pictures. You may want to get some guidelines for your guests. Ensure that the contract states that you are not obligated to pay for photos that do not turn out. Blurry photos, overexposed photos, underexposed photos, and prints without sufficient fix on them do not constitute photography worth paying for.

Friends or family members who are camcorder buffs can be of great assistance to you, too, even if unconsciously. One or two may simply show up with the camcorder and record your entire reception. Their home-movie approach may turn out to be far more entertaining than the polished production of the pro, if you hired one. Ask them to send you a copy (or the original, and return the copy to them.)

As you can see from all of the above information, the reception is a major part of the wedding preparation. But don't worry; the guide sheets provided in this book will help you sort through the details and to make your reception a fitting conclusion to a beautiful wedding.

CHAPTER NINE

Love, Caring and Thank-You Writing

Quick Response

rite a personal, signed, thank-you note for all gifts received, no matter how impressive or apparently insignificant, even if you have already thanked the presenter in person.

🖎 Send the thank-you note promptly. If this is not possible, send an acknowledgment (see below).

WEDDING-GIFT RECORD

To cope with the project simply and efficiently, use the *Guest List and Gifts Received* guides in this book.

Record each gift immediately, taking care to check the address on the mailing package. You may want a bridesmaid to do this for you as you open the gifts. If you wait until later, cards and gifts can be separated and cause confusion!

Preprinted Gift Acknowledgments

Your (and your fiancé's) prospective wedding guests; wedding party; volunteer helpers; as well as friends and family who throw bridal showers, dinners and other parties may amount to 600 people. Because response time is always important, you could purchase preprinted gift acknowledgments when you order your wedding stationery. To save time later, you could pre-address and sign these cards as soon as the gifts arrive. Or sign them ahead of time and have family send them for you while you're on your honeymoon.

Your acknowledgments may be more warmly received if you and your fiancé sign them together than if you signed them yourself. There is a reason for this. You may not know the same people, and personal acknowledgment from someone a person knows is more meaningful than from someone one does not know. Following this advice will be especially rewarding for you if this is a second wedding in which children (of any age) are involved.

You may consider the possibility that gifts will arrive on your doorstep long before the wedding. These gifts require the same immediate response as those received the week of the wedding. You will not want to use your married name when you respond to those gifts, so use both your name and your husband's, as you see in the following sample. These could be hand-written to save the cost of printing.

Sample Copy

June Lang and Myron Severson
wish to acknowledge the receipt
of your lovely wedding gift.
A personal, written thank you
will be sent later.

Share Your Joy and Create
a Lasting Impression

This is the message the bride needs to communicate to the people who have participated in her wedding celebration: For all that you are, for what you have done, I love you. In a simple, elegant and endearing way, your thank-you notes will honor the giver for all of the thought, time, effort and money put into the gift. Written in your own words and by your own hand, the notes will convey your heart-felt sentiments in just the right way.

Formal Thank-You Notes

The traditional, 4" x 5" thank-you note, called an "informal," is ordered with the wedding invitations. These engraved cards match the engraved wedding stationery. The customary ink color is black, but contemporary brides often select gold, silver, gray, blue, maroon or rose. Ask the printer for samples to look at before you make your final decision.

Semiformal and Informal Thank-You Notes

No matter how informal your wedding, select cards

that are blank on the inside. You may discover that your local stationer or greeting-card distributor has a fairly good selection of note cards from which to choose. Customarily, you would choose one with the words "Thank You" on the cover. You could choose a card that has wedding bells or some other typical wedding symbol on the cover and no words at all.

General Guidelines for Thank-You Writing

LEGIBILITY AND CLARITY

For the sake of your recipients, use either black or blue ink when you write and sign your thank-you notes. Write as legibly as you can, and be sure that your handwriting is large and clear enough for readers who cannot see well. You do not need to write more than a few lines to make your gratitude understood. Make the card dignified in appearance and warm in sentiment.

BE YOURSELF

No matter how flowery or impressive, no one else's words are as appropriate as your own. Please do not copy someone else's form letter, simply inserting the name of the individual and description of the gift. Your grandmother will know if you are expressing your own feelings, and so will your close friends. To let them know how much you really care, do your own writing.

If you have maintained your wedding *Guest List and Gifts Received Guides* (see guides in the last half of this book) and paid close attention to them, you would do well to thank the givers in person — casually, when you see them again.

CHAPTER TEN

Honeymoon: Prologue to Your New Life

Costs to Consider

His and Hers honeymoon trousseaus ❧ Luggage ❧ Package honeymoon-vacation deals ❧ On-your-own deals ❧ Airfares and airport taxes ❧ Car rentals ❧ Taxi fares ❧ Train, bus, or ship-line fares ❧ Eurailpass or Eurail Flexipass (for first-class train travel through 17 European countries) ❧ Hotels, resorts, lodges ❧ Restaurants ❧ Pampering (facials and manicuring, tanning at salons, health-spa workouts and steam baths, sports-club tennis and racquetball, etc.) ❧ Shopping ❧ Sightseeing tours ❧ Laundry ❧ Telephone calls and telegrams ❧ Gratuities and cover charges

Travel Agencies

Unless either you or your fiancé are very familiar

with your honeymoon destination, you need seasoned, experienced advice from someone who is. Travel agents may be able to find honeymoon discounts for you that might be overlooked if you plan on your own. You may need recommendations in order to find the perfect travel agent. Ask your friends, recommendations from those who actually availed themselves of travel-agency services for their honeymoons. Otherwise, consult the Yellow Pages of your phone book.

WHAT TO EXPECT FROM YOUR TRAVEL AGENT

‰ Information, suggestions and review of all necessary details (passport, visa, immunizations, if you need to carry a driver's license with photo identification, a notarized birth certificate, a voter-registration card, marriage license, airline restrictions such as luggage weight and number, etc.) ‰ Diligent effort to provide a superior honeymoon package value at a superior rate ‰ Itinerary ‰ Tickets and transfer coupons ‰ Hotel/ Motel/ Resort / Lodge confirmations ‰ Sightseeing vouchers

If you need passports, make your application for a passport at a county government center or federal passport office. Take your birth certificates (or naturalization certificate) with you when you apply; they will serve as your proof of citizenship. Also have your drivers' licenses with you for proof of identify. Two identical passport photos for each of you (2" x 2" head shots, either black-and-white or in color) will also be required. After you have made the application for passports, allow four weeks before receipt. If you do not have a month to wait for the passports, you could get them through a federal passport office. In that case, be prepared to wait in a long line for service; and be sure you have all of the information you need when you get to the head of the line.

For you, the bride, a passport requires special consideration. If your honeymoon is scheduled to begin less than a month from your wedding date, you will not be able to obtain a passport in your married name unless you go to a federal passport office. This means that you should expect to obtain your passport in your maiden name. Your traveler's checks should also be in your maiden name so that when you cash them, your passport will serve as your proof of identity.

OTHER INFORMATION AND IDENTIFICATION TO TAKE WITH YOU

꿈 Your travel agent's phone number (including emergency phone numbers), fax number and address 꿈 List of luggage and contents for claim purposes (you may fly to New York City, while your luggage flies to San Francisco) 꿈 Drivers' licenses 꿈 Marriage license 꿈 Address book (including emergency information: family doctor's name, clinic address, day and night phone numbers; allergies, blood types, medical warnings; both sets of parents' addresses and phone numbers; friends or relatives in honeymoon area, including phone numbers) 꿈 health insurance card, group policy number, personal identification number, phone number to call 꿈 auto insurance card, address, policy number, agent's phone number 꿈 Prescriptions for medicine, glasses, etc. 꿈 List of traveler's check numbers ✣ MasterCard, Visa or American Express credit cards (including list of all credit-card numbers) ✣ Instant Cash card or phone number of family bank (banker's name, bank address, phone number, and perhaps the fax number) in case you need extra money (Call the U.S. Consulate if you are in trouble and need advice immediately.) ✣ Language dictionary ✣ Foreign currency and list of exchange rates.

Our

Wedding
Planning
Guides

Getting It Together

*Use this Guide to record the names of the people who will help you
in gathering important information for planning your wedding.
(ie. prices, availability, etc.)*

STATIONERY *(invitations, reception cards, thank-you notes,
napkins, programs, etc.)*

Name   Phone

MUSIC *(organizers, singers, instrumentalists, etc.)*

Name   Phone

FLORAL ARRANGEMENTS AND DECORATIONS

Name   Phone

PHOTOGRAPHY AND VIDEO

Name   Phone

WEDDING ATTIRE

Name   Phone

EQUIPMENT DELIVERY AND PICK UP

Name   Phone

TRANSPORTATION

Name   Phone

GUEST REGISTRY

Name   Phone

MENU AND FOOD PREPARATION

Name   Phone

RECEPTION ORGANIZER

Name   Phone

RECEPTION SERVING *(pour coffee, cut cake, replenish serving trays, etc.)*

Name   Phone

Budget

First, determine what will meet your expectations. Then, use the following percentage estimates for the bride's total wedding budget. You should alter these percentages to emphasize the elements that are most important to you.

CATEGORY	PERCENTAGE OF TOTAL
Ceremony and Reception	50%
Flowers	8%
Stationery	4%
Music	4%
Photography and Video	11%
Rentals	1%
Wedding Attire	15%
Thank You Gifts	2%
Transportation	2%
Other	3%
Total	100%

Sample

If your budget is $10,000 and you want an appropriate figure for photography and video, multiply the total budget amount of $10,000 by 11% and enter that amount on the Bride's Budget worksheet.

$10,000 x .11= $1,100

After having computed the amounts for each category, you may want to revaluate your priorities. Make whatever adjustments necessary to more closely meet your expectations.

Your fiancé can work out a similar set of percentages for his budget and enter the amounts on the Groom's Budget worksheet.

Keep all of your receipts and contracts in a safe place. In order to locate them at the appropriate time, we suggest that you categorize them and place them in separate, marked envelopes.

Traditional Bride's Budget

BUDGETED ITEMS	AMOUNT BUDGETED	TOTAL COST	DEPOSIT	BALANCE DUE
STATIONERY:	_____	_____		
Invitations		_____	_____	_____
Reception Cards		_____	_____	_____
Response Cards		_____	_____	_____
Map		_____	_____	_____
Thank-You Notes		_____	_____	_____
Napkins		_____	_____	_____
Matches		_____	_____	_____
Programs		_____	_____	_____
Announcements		_____	_____	_____
BRIDAL ATTIRE	_____	_____		
Dress		_____	_____	_____
Headpiece & Veil		_____	_____	_____
Shoes		_____	_____	_____
Accessories		_____	_____	_____
GROOM'S WEDDING RING & GIFT:	_____	_____	_____	_____
BRIDAL ATTENDANT'S GIFTS:	_____	_____	_____	_____
BRIDE'S MEDICAL	_____	_____	_____	_____
RECEPTION:	_____	_____		
Site Fee		_____	_____	_____
Caterer		_____	_____	_____
Food		_____	_____	_____

TRADITIONAL BRIDE'S BUDGET CONTINUED

BUDGETED ITEMS	AMOUNT BUDGETED	TOTAL COST	DEPOSIT DUE	BALANCE
Beverages				
Gratuity & Tax				
Cake				
Additional Services				
MUSIC:				
Ceremony				
Reception				
FLORIST:				
Ceremony Site Flowers				
Bridesmaids' Bouquets				
Groom's Boutonniere				
Fathers' Boutonnieres				
Grandfathers' Boutonnieres				
Reception Site Flowers				
Special Others				
Other				
PHOTOGRAPHERS:				
Formal Portraits				
Engagement				
Wedding				
Wedding Package				
Parents' Album				
Extra Pictures				

TRADITIONAL BRIDE'S BUDGET CONTINUED

BUDGETED ITEMS	AMOUNT BUDGETED	TOTAL COST	DEPOSIT	BALANCE DUE
VIDEOTAPING:				
AUDIOTAPING:				
SPECIAL PARTIES:	_____	_____		
Bridal Luncheon		_____	_____	_____
Pre-Ceremony Buffet		_____	_____	_____
RENTAL EQUIPMENT	_____	_____		
Ceremony		_____	_____	_____
Reception		_____	_____	_____
TRANSPORTATION:	_____	_____		
Parking Attendant		_____	_____	_____
Car Rental		_____	_____	_____
MISCELLANEOUS FEES	_____	_____		
Ceremony Site Fee		_____	_____	_____
Wedding Coordinator		_____	_____	_____
Maid Service		_____	_____	_____
Guard for Home		_____	_____	_____
Temporary Insurance Policy		_____	_____	_____
Other _____		_____	_____	_____
_____		_____	_____	_____

Traditional Groom's Budget

BUDGETED ITEMS	AMOUNT BUDGETED	TOTAL COST	DEPOSIT	BALANCE DUE
WEDDING ATTIRE	_____	_____		
Groom		_____	_____	_____
Mother		_____	_____	_____
Father		_____	_____	_____
Other		_____	_____	_____
HOUSING/ TRANSPORTATION:	_____	_____	_____	_____
RINGS:	_____	_____		
Engagement		_____	_____	_____
Wedding		_____	_____	_____
GIFT FOR THE BRIDE:	_____	_____	_____	_____
ATTENDANT'S GIFTS:	_____	_____	_____	_____
MEDICAL:	_____	_____	_____	_____
FLOWERS:	_____	_____		
Bride's Bouquet & Corsage		_____	_____	_____
Mothers' Corsages		_____	_____	_____
Grandmothers' Corsages		_____	_____	_____
Ushers' Boutonnieres		_____	_____	_____

TRADITIONAL GROOM'S BUDGET CONTINUED

BUDGETED ITEMS	AMOUNT BUDGETED	TOTAL COST	DEPOSIT	BALANCE DUE
BACHELOR'S PARTY:	_____	_____	_____	_____
REHEARSAL DINNER:	_____	_____	_____	_____
HONEYMOON EXPENSES: *(Include an additional 10% to cover unexpected expenses.)*	_____	_____	_____	_____
MARRIAGE LICENSE:	_____	_____	_____	_____
OFFICIANT'S FEE:	_____	_____	_____	_____
OTHER: _____	_____	_____	_____	_____
_____	_____	_____	_____	_____
_____	_____	_____	_____	_____
_____	_____	_____	_____	_____
_____	_____	_____	_____	_____
_____	_____	_____	_____	_____
_____	_____	_____	_____	_____
_____	_____	_____	_____	_____
_____	_____	_____	_____	_____
_____	_____	_____	_____	_____
_____	_____	_____	_____	_____
_____	_____	_____	_____	_____

Ceremony Site

Site _____

Address _____

Contact person _____ Phone _____

_____

	Rehearsal:	*Wedding:*
Available dates:	_____	_____
Time preference:	_____	_____
Confirmed:	_____	_____

Questions about facilities and regulations:

1. How many guests can the site accommodate?_____

2. When is the site available for rehearsal?_____

3. What are the church requirements for marriage?_____

_____

4. What, if any, are the regulations concerning the day or
   time of day to hold the wedding?_____

_____

5. Are there other weddings on the same day? _____

6. Is there a possibility of another wedding being scheduled
   on that day? _____

7. Do special vows need to have approval? ☐ Yes ☐ No

8. What are the restrictions on music? _____

_____

9. What are the restrictions on decorations? Flowers?_____

_____

10. What accessories does the site provide and what are the
fees for using the accessories? _____

_____

CEREMONY SITE CONTINUED

☐ Candelabra $_____   ☐ Candles $_____
☐ Candlelighters $_____   ☐ Arch $_____
☐ Kneeling Bench $_____   ☐ Flower stands $_____
☐ Guestbook Stand $_____

11. What are the rules regarding photography?_____

12. Is there a designated room for the photographer to take pictures? ☐ Yes   ☐ No

13. Is there a sound system for recording the wedding?
☐ Yes ☐ No Fee for use? $_____ Cost for copies? $_____

14. Are there facilities for the bridal party? ☐ Yes   ☐ No
Restrooms? ☐ Yes   ☐ No
Designated room for the bride? ☐ Yes   ☐ No

15. What is the fee for the use of the building? $_____
For the custodian? $_____

16. What are the additional charges for using the site as a reception? $_____

Notes:_____

_____
_____
_____
_____
_____
_____
_____
_____
_____
_____
_____

Floral Guidelines

Florist _____

Address _____

Contact person _____ Phone _____

Appt. Date _____ Time _____

Ceremony Flowers

Qty.   Cost   *Description (color, size, type):*

BRIDE:

____ ____ Bouquet _____

_____

____ ____ Small Bouquet for throwing_____

_____

____ ____ Going-away corsage_____

_____

BRIDAL ATTENDANTS:

____ ____ Honor Attendant's bouquet _____

_____

name: _____

____ ____ Bridesmaid's bouquet _____

_____

names: _____

_____

_____

_____

_____

____ ____ Flower Girl's bouquet/basket _____

_____

name: _____

FLORAL GUIDELINES CONTINUED

Qty.   *Cost*   *Description (color, size, type):*

____ _____ Floral Headdresses _____

_____

GROOM & ATTENDANTS

____ _____ Groom's boutonniere _____

_____

____ _____ Best Man's boutonniere _____

_____

____ _____ Groomsmen/Ushers' boutonnieres _____

_____

names: _____

_____

_____

_____

_____

____ _____ Ring Bearer's boutonniere _____

_____

*name:*_____

MOTHERS AND GRANDMOTHERS

_____

____ _____ Mother of the Bride corsage _____

_____

*name:*_____

____ _____ Mother of the Groom corsage _____

_____

*name:*_____

____ _____ Mothers' roses _____

_____

FLORAL GUIDELINES CONTINUED

Qty.   Cost   *Description (color, size, type):*

____ _____ Grandmothers' corsage_____

_____

*names:*_____

_____

_____

_____

____ _____ Other Corsages *(stepmothers, foster mothers, etc.)*

_____

*names:*_____

_____

_____

_____

FATHERS AND GRANDFATHERS

____ _____ Father of the Bride boutonniere_____

_____

name: _____

____ _____ Father of the Groom boutonniere _____

_____

name: _____

____ _____ Other Boutonnieres *(stepfathers, foster fathers, etc.)*

_____

*names:*_____

_____

_____

_____

_____

FLORAL GUIDELINES CONTINUED

Qty. *Cost* *Description (color, size, type):*

____ _____ Grandfathers' boutonniere _____

_____

names: _____

_____

_____

_____

_____

ALTAR

____ _____ Arch/Canopy_____

_____

____ _____ Kneeling bench _____

_____

____ _____ Candelabra: _____

_____

____ _____ Candlelighters _____

____ _____ Candles (color) _____

____ _____ Floral sprays _____

____ _____ Beauty vases _____

____ _____ Potted flowers _____

____ _____ Potted plants _____

____ _____ Potted trees _____

____ _____ Plant stands _____

____ _____ Other: _____

AISLE

____ _____ Pew decorations _____

_____

FLORAL GUIDELINES CONTINUED

Qty.   *Cost*   *Description (color, size, type):*

____   _____ Candelabra _____

____   _____ Candles (color) _____

____   _____ Floral arrangements _____

____   _____ Greenery and bows _____

____   _____ Aisle ribbons _____

____   _____ Aisle runner *(length,color)* _____

____   _____ Other :_____

OTHERS FOR WHOM YOU MAY WISH TO PROVIDE FLOWERS

____   _____ Soloist(s)_____

*name:(s)*_____

____   _____ Officiant_____

name: _____

____   _____ Guestbook attendant(s)_____

*name:(s)*_____

____   _____ Gift attendant(s) _____

*name:(s)*_____

____   _____ Cake servers_____

*name:(s)*_____

____   _____ Hospitality committee_____

*name:(s)*_____

____   _____ Others _____

*name:(s)*_____

_____

_____

_____

_____

_____

FLORAL GUIDELINES CONTINUED

Reception Flowers

Qty.	Cost	Description (color, size, type):

TABLE CENTERPIECES:

____ _____ Bride's Table _____

____ _____ Parents' Table _____

____ _____ Attendants' Table(s)_____

____ _____ Guest Tables _____

____ _____ Other: _____

OTHER DECORATIONS:

____ _____ Table garlands_____

____ _____ Top of cake_____

____ _____ Around cake_____

____ _____ Receiving line area _____

____ _____ Guestbook stand_____

____ _____ Table for receiving gifts_____

____ _____ Ladies' powder room _____

____ _____ Other: _____

____ _____ _____

____ _____ _____

Service Costs

FOR THE CEREMONY:

Delivery $ _____

Setup   _____

Removal   _____

Other   _____

FOR THE RECEPTION:

Delivery $ _____

Setup   _____

Removal   _____

Other   _____

Floral Diagrams

AISLE AND ALTAR

Floral Diagrams

(For the placement of flowers, plants, and various decorations)

ENTRY AREA

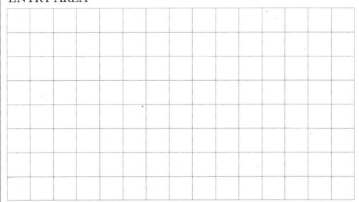

RECEPTION SITE
(Including guestbook stand or table, and gift table)

Wedding Invitations

Wording: _____

_____

_____

_____

_____

_____

Quantity: _____

Supplier _____

  Phone _____ Bid _____

Supplier _____

  Phone _____ Bid _____

Supplier _____

  Phone _____ Bid _____

Supplier _____

  Phone _____ Bid _____

Estimated Cost _____ Actual Cost _____

Time Needed _____

Date Ordered _____ Date Received _____

Date Sent _____

Choosing Your Music

PRELUDES/ PROCESSIONALS/ RECESSIONALS

BACH, J.S.

Adagio Cantabile

Adagio in A Minor

Air on G String

Andante from *Brandenburg Concerto No. 2*

Aria, "When Thou Art Near"

Arioso

In Thee Is Gladness

Jesu, Joy of Man's Desiring

My Heart Ever Faithful

Praise to the Lord, the Almighty

Prelude in D

Sarabande

Sheep May Safely Graze

Symphonia From Wedding Cantata, 195

BEETHOVEN, L.

Ode to Joy

BEILLMANN, L.

Priere a' Notre Dame

COUPERIN

Fanfare

DOANE, W.

To God Be the Glory

DUNSTABLE, J.

Agincourt Hymn

ELDRIDGE, G.H.

Fanfare

FRANCK, C.

Fantasie in C

GOSS, J.

Praise My Soul, the King of Heaven

HANDEL, G.F.

Andante Maestoso

Aria From Concerto Grosso XII

Aria in F Major

Hallelujah Chorus

Larghetto from *Water Music Suite*

Sarabande from *Suite No. 11*

KARG-ELERT, S.

Now Thank We All Our God

LISZT, F.

Adagio

LOHENGRIN

Bridal Chorus

MARCELLO, B.

Psalm XIX

Psalm XX

MENDELSSOHN, F.

Excerpts From Organ Sonatas

First Organ Sonata

War March of the Priests

PACHELBEL, J.

Cannon in D

Pastorale

PEETERS, F.

Abide, O Dearest Jesus

CHOOSING YOUR MUSIC CONTINUED

Awake, My Heart, With
Gladness

Ten Preludes on Old Flemish
Tunes

PURCELL, H.

Bell Symphony

Largo in D Major

March in C

Trumpet Tune in C

Trumpet Tune in D

Trumpet Tune in D Major

Trumpet Voluntary in D

Trumpet Voluntary in D Major

SCHUBERT

Ave Maria

TCHAIKOVSKY

Apotheosis

Vangelis

Theme from Chariots of Fire

VIVALDI

Spring from *The Four Seasons*

HYMNS/VOCALS

A Wedding Blessing,
Austin Lovelace

A Wedding Prayer, *Williams*

All Creatures of Our God and
King, St. *Francis of Assisi*

Be Thou My (Our) Vision,
Ancient Irish

Be Thou With Them, *J.S. Bach*

Bridal Prayer, *Copeland*

The Call, *R. Vaughan-Williams*

Children of the Heavenly Father,
Lina Sandell

Day by Day, *Lina Sandell Berg*

Entreat Me Not to Leave Thee,
C.F. Gounod

Evergreen, *Barbra Streisand*

Fairest Lord Jesus,
from *the German*

Flesh of My Flesh, *Patillo*

For the Beauty of the Earth,
F.S. Pierpoint

God of Our Life, Through All the
Circling Years, *Hugh T. Kerr*

The God of Love My Shepherd Is,
E. Thiman

The Greatest of These Is Love,
R. Bitgood

Happy the Home, *Henry Ware*

Heart Full of Love, *Boubil,
Schonberg, and Kretzmer*

Here at Thine Altar, Lord,
A. Rowley

Here We Are Now, *Purifoy*

Household of Faith, *Lamb, Rosasco*

I Love Thee, *Grieg*

If With All Your Hearts,
F. Mendelssohn

In This Very Room, *Harris*

Jesu, Joy of Man's Desiring,
J.S. Bach

Jesus, Guest at Cana's Wedding,
Peterson

CHOOSING YOUR MUSIC CONTINUED

Jesus, Lead Our Footsteps Ever,
J.S. Bach

Jesus, Shepherd, Be Thou Near
Me, *J.S. Bach*

Joyful, Joyful We Adore Thee,
Henry van Dyke

Keep Us One, *Johnson, D.*

The King of Love My Shepherd Is,
Bairstow

Like a River Glorious,
Frances Havergal

Like a Shepherd God Doth Lead
Us, *J.S. Bach*

The Lord's Prayer, *Regina H.
Fryxell; also Ley*

Love Divine, *B. Marcello*

Love Divine, All Loves Excelling,
Charles Wesley

Make Us One, *Johnson, P.*

May the Grace of Christ Our
Saviour, *John Newton*

May the Mind of Christ My (Our)
Saviour, *Kate B. Wilkinson*

Me and My House, *Sheppard*

My Heart, Ever Faithful, *J.S. Bach*

Now Thank We All Our God,
Martin Rinkart

O Lord Most Holy, *Caesar Franck*

O Love That Casts Out Fear,
J.S. Bach

O Love That Wilt Not Let Me Go,
Hudstad

O Perfect Love, *Dorothy Gurney;*

Oh, Blest the House Whate're
Befall, *Henry Markworth*

One Hand, One Heart,
Bernstein and Sondheim

Only God Would Love You
More, *Liles, Borop*

Our Love, *Scott, Coomes, North*

Praise, My Soul, the King of
Heaven, *Henry F. Lyte*

Psalm 150, *Ned Rorem*

Saviour, Like a shepherd Lead
Us, *Dorothy A. Thrupp*

Set Me as a Seal Upon Thine
Heart, *Joseph Clokey*

Sunrise, Sunset, *Harnick, Bock*

This Is the Day (or, A Wedding
Song), *Brown*

Thou Art Like a Flower, *Schumann*

Thou Wilt Keep Him in Perfect
Peace, *E. Thiman*

Though I Speak With the
Tongues, *J. Brahms*

Time for Joy, *Limpic*

We Come, O Christ, to Thee,
Margaret Clarkson

We Lift Our Hearts to Thee,
A. Lovelace

We Rest on Thee,
Edith G. Cherry

Wedding Song, *H. Schultz*

When You Created Love, *Fettke*

Wither Thou Goest,
G. Winston Cassler

Music Estimates

Ceremony _____ Hours needed _____

Reception _____ Hours needed _____

_____

Musician/Agent _____ Phone _____

Address _____

Rate per hour _____ Overtime rate per hour _____

Number of rest breaks _____

Audition Date _____ Time _____

Place _____

Note: _____

Chosen?   ☐ Yes   ☐ No

_____

Musician/Agent _____ Phone _____

Address _____

Rate per hour _____ Overtime rate per hour _____

Number of rest breaks _____

Audition Date _____ Time _____

Place _____

Note: _____

Chosen?   ☐ Yes   ☐ No

_____

Musician/Agent _____ Phone _____

Address _____

Rate per hour _____ Overtime rate per hour _____

Number of rest breaks _____

Audition Date _____ Time _____

Place _____

Note: _____

Chosen?   ☐ Yes   ☐ No

Ceremony Music

CEREMONY SITE

Contact person _____ Phone _____

Appointment date _____ Time: _____ Place: _____

Instrumentalists: _____ Phone _____

_____

_____

_____

_____

Soloists: _____ Phone _____

_____

_____

Music Sequence:	Selection:	Musician
Prelude		

_____

_____

_____

Processional _____

_____

_____

_____

_____

Recessional _____

_____

_____

Postlude _____

Photographer's Guidelines

Engagement pictures:
_____

Time   Date   Place
_____

Formal bridal portrait:
_____

Time   Date   Place
_____

Guidelines/Ceremony site restrictions
_____

_____

Suggested formal shots:

BRIDE	GROOM
____ alone	____ alone
with:	*with:*
____ father	____ father
____ mother	____ mother
____ parents	____ parents
____ Maid of Honor	____ Best Man
____ Bridesmaids	____ Groomsmen/Ushers
____ Flower Girl	____ Ring Bearer
____ Grandparents	____ Grandparents
____ Family	____ Family
____ _____	____ _____
____ _____	____ _____
____ _____	____ _____
____ _____	____ _____
____ _____	____ _____
____ _____	____ _____
____ _____	____ _____
____ _____	____ _____
____ _____	____ _____

PHOTOGRAPHER'S GUIDELINES CONTINUED

BRIDE & GROOM
____ together
with:
____ Best Man
____ Maid of Honor
____ Honor Attendants
____ Bridesmaids
____ Groomsmen/Ushers
____ Flower Girl &
     Ring Bearer
____ Grandparents
____ Both families
____ Bridal Party
____ Bride's Parents
____ Groom's Parents
____ Officiant
____ _____
____ _____
____ _____

Suggested shots at the reception:
____ Arrival
____ Cutting the cake
____ Cake table
____ Food table
____ The toast
____ Bridal Table
____ Reception line
____ Bride throwing bouquet
____ Bride & Groom feeding
     each other cake

Suggested miscellaneous shots
____ The rings
____ Lighting Unity Candle

Videotaping

FIRST CHOICE	SECOND CHOICE
Name	Name
Address	Address
Phone	Phone
Contact	Contact
Appt. date/time	Appt. date/time
SERVICES OFFERED	SERVICES OFFERED
Number of hours taping	Number of hours taping
Tape length:	Tape length
Number of cassettes	Number of cassettes
Number of cameras	Number of cameras
Editing	Editing
Audio capability	Audio capability
Dubbing	Dubbing
Special effects	Special effects
Extra cassettes:	Extra cassettes:
Additional services *(list below)*	Additional services *(list below)*
COST	COST

Photographer chosen

Date contract signed

Total cost   Deposit paid

Balance due   Date due

Payment made by: ☐ credit card   ☐ cash/check

Date video will be ready

Equipment

Rental Agency _____

Address _____

Contact _____ Phone _____

Qty.	Cost	
		CEREMONY:
____	_____	Wedding arch
____	_____	Wedding canopy
____	_____	Backdrops
		FLOOR CANDELABRA:
____	_____	3-light
____	_____	7-light
____	_____	9-light
____	_____	15-light, spiral
____	_____	17-light, heartshape
		AISLE CANDELABRA:
____	_____	Clamp
____	_____	Free-standing
____	_____	Candles (color:)
____	_____	Candlelighters
____	_____	Kneeling bench
____	_____	Aisle stanchions
____	_____	Aisle runner (length:)
____	_____	Floral baskets

Qty.	Cost	
		FLOWER STANDS:
____	_____	8"
____	_____	12"
____	_____	16"
____	_____	20"
____	_____	24"
____	_____	Guest book stand
		CHAIRS:
____	_____	padded folding chairs
____	_____	unpadded folding chairs
		OBLONG TABLES: _30" wide, 29" high)_
____	_____	6' (6-8 people)
____	_____	8' (8-10 people)
		ROUND TABLES:
____	_____	36" diameter (4 people)
____	_____	48" diameter (6 people)
____	_____	60" diameter (8 people)
____	_____	72" diameter (10 to 12 people)
____	_____	card tables

EQUIPMENT CONTINUED

Qty.	Cost	

SQUARE LINENS:

____ ____ 54" x 54"
(card table)

____ ____ 60" x 60"
(card table)

LONG LINENS:

____ ____ 60" x 120"
(6' and 8' tables)

ROUND LINENS:

____ ____ 60" diameter
(24" to 36" round tables)

____ ____ 72" diameter
(24" to 48" round tables; drapes 24" to floor)

____ ____ 90" diameter
(36" to 60" round tables; drapes 36" to floor)

____ ____ 100" diameter
(48" to 72" round tables; drapes 48" to floor)

____ ____ 120" diameter
(60" to 72" round table; drapes 60" to floor)

NAPKINS:

____ ____ Cocktail

____ ____ Dinner

Qty.	Cost	

TABLE SKIRTING:

____ ____ 6' table, 4 sides: 204" + overlap

____ ____ 6' table, 3 sides: 132" + overlap

____ ____ 8' table, 4 sides: 252" + overlap

____ ____ 60" round table: 189" + overlap

____ ____ 72" round table: 227" + overlap

____ ____ 90" round table: 283" + plus overlap

____ ____ 100" round table: 314" plus overlap

____ ____ 120" round table: 377" plus overlap

GLASSWARE:

☐ Glass   ☐ Plastic

STEMWARE:

____ ____ 4 1/2 oz. glass

____ ____ 6 1/2 oz. glass

____ ____ 12 oz. water goblet

____ ____ Parfait glass

____ ____ Sherbet glass

EQUIPMENT CONTINUED

Qty.   Cost

GLASSES:

___ _____ 4 oz. punch cup

___ _____ 5 oz. juice glass

___ _____ 8 oz. water glass

___ _____ Pitchers

DINNERWARE:

☐ China   ☐ Glass   ☐ Plastic

___ _____ Dinner plates

___ _____ Salad plates

___ _____ Bread and butter Plates

___ _____ Cups

___ _____ Saucers

___ _____ Soup bowls

___ _____ Fruit bowls

___ _____ Creamer and sugar sets

___ _____ Salt and pepper shaker sets

___ _____ Vegetable bowls

___ _____ Gravy boats

___ _____ Platters

FLATWARE:

☐ Silverplate   ☐ Stainless

___ _____ Dinner knives

___ _____ Dinner forks

Qty.   Cost

___ _____ Teaspoons

___ _____ Salad and dessert forks

___ _____ Soup spoons

___ _____ Butter knives

___ _____ Shrimp forks

___ _____ Steak knives

___ _____ Meat forks

___ _____ Salad spoon and fork sets

___ _____ Salad tongs

___ _____ Serving spoons

___ _____ Cake knife

___ _____ Cake server

PUNCH FOUNTAINS:

___ _____ 3-gallon

___ _____ 7-gallon

PUNCH BOWLS

☐ Silver   ☐ Glass   ☐ Plastic

___ _____ With tray

___ _____ Without tray

___ _____ Silver ladle

___ _____ Plastic ladle

COFFEE MAKERS AND SERVERS:

___ _____ Automatic:

___ _____ 35-cup

EQUIPMENT CONTINUED

Qty.	Cost	
____	____	55-cup
____	____	100-cup
____	____	Silver urns:
____	____	25-cup
____	____	50-cup
____	____	Tray
____	____	Sugar and creamer sets
____	____	Silver coffee and tea service *(2 pots, tray, sugar and creamer)*
____	____	Insulated coffee pitchers

OTHER SERVING PIECES:

Qty.	Cost	
____	____	Silver relish dishes
____	____	Silver bonbon dishes
____	____	Silver bread dishes
____	____	Silver sugar tongs

CHAFING DISHES:

☐ Silver   ☐ Stainless

Qty.	Cost	
____	____	2-quart

Qty.	Cost	
____	____	4-quart
____	____	8-quart

FOOD PANS:

Full pan:

| ____ | ____ | 4-quart |
| ____ | ____ | 8-quart |

1/2 pan:

| ____ | ____ | 4-quart |
| ____ | ____ | 8-quart |

1/3 pan:

| ____ | ____ | 4-quart |
| ____ | ____ | 8-quart |

BOWLS:

☐ Stainless   ☐ Plastic

____	____	12"
____	____	14"
____	____	16"
____	____	18"
____	____	20"
____	____	24"
____	____	Electric roasters
____	____	Electric hotplates:
____	____	Single burner
____	____	Double burner

EQUIPMENT CONTINUED

Qty.	Cost	

TRAYS:

☐ Silver   ☐ Chrome

☐ Stainless   ☐ Plastic

Qty.	Cost	
____	_____	10" round
____	_____	12" round
____	_____	14" round
____	_____	16" round
____	_____	18" round
____	_____	20" round
____	_____	22" round
____	_____	13" x 21" oval
____	_____	15" x 24" oval
____	_____	10" x 17" oblong
____	_____	13" x 19" oblong
____	_____	14" x 22" oblong
____	_____	17" x 23" oblong
____	_____	Waiters' trays

FLOORS AND STAGES:

____	_____	Floors

(Generally 4' x 4' wood sections. Divide square footage of area to be covered by square footage of one section of wood to determine number of sections required.)
Stages (Generally 3' x 6' sections)

LIGHTING AND ELECTRICAL:

Qty.	Cost	
____	_____	Spotlights
____	_____	Pole lights
____	_____	Twinkle lights
____	_____	Extension cords
____	_____	Other

(list other equipment below)

――	――	――――――
――	――	――――――
――	――	――――――
――	――	――――――
――	――	――――――
――	――	――――――
――	――	――――――
――	――	――――――
――	――	――――――
――	――	――――――
――	――	――――――
――	――	――――――
――	――	――――――

HEATING:

____	_____	Indoor electric heaters
____	_____	Outdoor propane heaters

EQUIPMENT CONTINUED

Qty.	Cost	
		COOLING:
____	_____	Floor fans
____	_____	Table fans
		CANOPIES:
____	_____	Canopies
____	_____	Umbrellas
____	_____	Sidewalls for canopies

GUEST EQUIPMENT:

____ _____ Rollaway beds:

☐ 30"   ☐ 39"   ☐ 48"

____ _____ Baby crib

____ _____ High chair

____ _____ Playpen

OTHER EQUIPMENT:

____ _____ Garbage cans

____ _____ Movie Projector

____ _____ Slide Projector

____ _____ Projector Screen

Qty.   Cost
(list other equipment below)

____ _____ _____

____ _____ _____

____ _____ _____

____ _____ _____

____ _____ _____

____ _____ _____

____ _____ _____

____ _____ _____

____ _____ _____

____ _____ _____

____ _____ _____

____ _____ _____

Date rental contract signed

Total cost _____

Deposit paid _____

Balance due _____

Date Due _____

Payment made by:_____

☐ credit card ☐ cash/check

Equipment Delivery & Return

Name

Address

Contact person   Phone

CEREMONY SITE:

Before:

Contact person   Phone

Date   Time

Pickup

Delivery

Setup

Payment   When

After:

Date When Due   Time

Tear Down   By Whom

Return   By Whom

RECEPTION SITE:

Before:

Contact person   Phone

Date   Time

Pickup

Delivery

Setup

Payment   When

After:

Date When Due   Time

Tear Down   By Whom

Return   By Whom

Bride's Guest List & Gifts Recd.

NAME: _____ Phone: _____

Address: _____

City,St. & Zip _____ Gift Rec'd: _____

NAME: _____ Phone: _____

Address: _____

City,St. & Zip _____ Gift Rec'd: _____

NAME: _____ Phone: _____

Address: _____

City,St. & Zip _____ Gift Rec'd: _____

NAME: _____ Phone: _____

Address: _____

City,St. & Zip _____ Gift Rec'd: _____

NAME: _____ Phone: _____

Address: _____

City,St. & Zip _____ Gift Rec'd: _____

NAME: _____ Phone: _____

Address: _____

City,St. & Zip _____ Gift Rec'd: _____

NAME: _____ Phone: _____

Address: _____

City,St. & Zip _____ Gift Rec'd: _____

NAME: _____ Phone: _____

Address: _____

City,St. & Zip _____ Gift Rec'd: _____

NAME: _____ Phone: _____

Address: _____

City,St. & Zip _____ Gift Rec'd: _____

BRIDE'S GUEST LIST & GIFTS RECD. CONT.

NAME: _____ Phone: _____

Address: _____

City,St. & Zip _____ Gift Rec'd: _____

NAME: _____ Phone: _____

Address: _____

City,St. & Zip _____ Gift Rec'd: _____

NAME: _____ Phone: _____

Address: _____

City,St. & Zip _____ Gift Rec'd: _____

NAME: _____ Phone: _____

Address: _____

City,St. & Zip _____ Gift Rec'd: _____

NAME: _____ Phone: _____

Address: _____

City,St. & Zip _____ Gift Rec'd: _____

NAME: _____ Phone: _____

Address: _____

City,St. & Zip _____ Gift Rec'd: _____

NAME: _____ Phone: _____

Address: _____

City,St. & Zip _____ Gift Rec'd: _____

NAME: _____ Phone: _____

Address: _____

City,St. & Zip _____ Gift Rec'd: _____

NAME: _____ Phone: _____

Address: _____

City,St. & Zip _____ Gift Rec'd: _____

BRIDE'S GUEST LIST & GIFTS RECD. CONT.

NAME: _____ Phone: _____

Address: _____

City,St. & Zip _____ Gift Rec'd: _____

NAME: _____ Phone: _____

Address: _____

City,St. & Zip _____ Gift Rec'd: _____

NAME: _____ Phone: _____

Address: _____

City,St. & Zip _____ Gift Rec'd: _____

NAME: _____ Phone: _____

Address: _____

City,St. & Zip _____ Gift Rec'd: _____

NAME: _____ Phone: _____

Address: _____

City,St. & Zip _____ Gift Rec'd: _____

NAME: _____ Phone: _____

Address: _____

City,St. & Zip _____ Gift Rec'd: _____

NAME: _____ Phone: _____

Address: _____

City,St. & Zip _____ Gift Rec'd: _____

NAME: _____ Phone: _____

Address: _____

City,St. & Zip _____ Gift Rec'd: _____

NAME: _____ Phone: _____

Address: _____

City,St. & Zip _____ Gift Rec'd: _____

BRIDE'S GUEST LIST & GIFTS RECD. CONT.

NAME: _____ Phone: _____

Address: _____

City,St. & Zip _____ Gift Rec'd: _____

NAME: _____ Phone: _____

Address: _____

City,St. & Zip _____ Gift Rec'd: _____

NAME: _____ Phone: _____

Address: _____

City,St. & Zip _____ Gift Rec'd: _____

NAME: _____ Phone: _____

Address: _____

City,St. & Zip _____ Gift Rec'd: _____

NAME: _____ Phone: _____

Address: _____

City,St. & Zip _____ Gift Rec'd: _____

NAME: _____ Phone: _____

Address: _____

City,St. & Zip _____ Gift Rec'd: _____

NAME: _____ Phone: _____

Address: _____

City,St. & Zip _____ Gift Rec'd: _____

NAME: _____ Phone: _____

Address: _____

City,St. & Zip _____ Gift Rec'd: _____

NAME: _____ Phone: _____

Address: _____

City,St. & Zip _____ Gift Rec'd: _____

BRIDE'S GUEST LIST & GIFTS RECD. CONT.

NAME: _____ Phone: _____

Address: _____

City,St. & Zip _____ Gift Rec'd: _____

NAME: _____ Phone: _____

Address: _____

City,St. & Zip _____ Gift Rec'd: _____

NAME: _____ Phone: _____

Address: _____

City,St. & Zip _____ Gift Rec'd: _____

NAME: _____ Phone: _____

Address: _____

City,St. & Zip _____ Gift Rec'd: _____

NAME: _____ Phone: _____

Address: _____

City,St. & Zip _____ Gift Rec'd: _____

NAME: _____ Phone: _____

Address: _____

City,St. & Zip _____ Gift Rec'd: _____

NAME: _____ Phone: _____

Address: _____

City,St. & Zip _____ Gift Rec'd: _____

NAME: _____ Phone: _____

Address: _____

City,St. & Zip _____ Gift Rec'd: _____

NAME: _____ Phone: _____

Address: _____

City,St. & Zip _____ Gift Rec'd: _____

BRIDE'S GUEST LIST & GIFTS RECD. CONT.

NAME: _____ Phone: _____

Address: _____

City,St. & Zip _____ Gift Rec'd: _____

NAME: _____ Phone: _____

Address: _____

City,St. & Zip _____ Gift Rec'd: _____

NAME: _____ Phone: _____

Address: _____

City,St. & Zip _____ Gift Rec'd: _____

NAME: _____ Phone: _____

Address: _____

City,St. & Zip _____ Gift Rec'd: _____

NAME: _____ Phone: _____

Address: _____

City,St. & Zip _____ Gift Rec'd: _____

NAME: _____ Phone: _____

Address: _____

City,St. & Zip _____ Gift Rec'd: _____

NAME: _____ Phone: _____

Address: _____

City,St. & Zip _____ Gift Rec'd: _____

NAME: _____ Phone: _____

Address: _____

City,St. & Zip _____ Gift Rec'd: _____

NAME: _____ Phone: _____

Address: _____

City,St. & Zip _____ Gift Rec'd: _____

BRIDE'S GUEST LIST & GIFTS RECD. CONT.

NAME: _____ Phone: _____

Address: _____

City,St. & Zip _____ Gift Rec'd: _____

NAME: _____ Phone: _____

Address: _____

City,St. & Zip _____ Gift Rec'd: _____

NAME: _____ Phone: _____

Address: _____

City,St. & Zip _____ Gift Rec'd: _____

NAME: _____ Phone: _____

Address: _____

City,St. & Zip _____ Gift Rec'd: _____

NAME: _____ Phone: _____

Address: _____

City,St. & Zip _____ Gift Rec'd: _____

NAME: _____ Phone: _____

Address: _____

City,St. & Zip _____ Gift Rec'd: _____

NAME: _____ Phone: _____

Address: _____

City,St. & Zip _____ Gift Rec'd: _____

NAME: _____ Phone: _____

Address: _____

City,St. & Zip _____ Gift Rec'd: _____

NAME: _____ Phone: _____

Address: _____

City,St. & Zip _____ Gift Rec'd: _____

BRIDE'S GUEST LIST & GIFTS RECD. CONT.

NAME: _____ Phone: _____

Address: _____

City, St. & Zip _____ Gift Rec'd: _____

NAME: _____ Phone: _____

Address: _____

City, St. & Zip _____ Gift Rec'd: _____

NAME: _____ Phone: _____

Address: _____

City, St. & Zip _____ Gift Rec'd: _____

NAME: _____ Phone: _____

Address: _____

City, St. & Zip _____ Gift Rec'd: _____

NAME: _____ Phone: _____

Address: _____

City, St. & Zip _____ Gift Rec'd: _____

NAME: _____ Phone: _____

Address: _____

City, St. & Zip _____ Gift Rec'd: _____

NAME: _____ Phone: _____

Address: _____

City, St. & Zip _____ Gift Rec'd: _____

NAME: _____ Phone: _____

Address: _____

City, St. & Zip _____ Gift Rec'd: _____

NAME: _____ Phone: _____

Address: _____

City, St. & Zip _____ Gift Rec'd: _____

BRIDE'S GUEST LIST & GIFTS RECD. CONT.

NAME: _____ Phone: _____

Address: _____

City,St. & Zip _____ Gift Rec'd: _____

NAME: _____ Phone: _____

Address: _____

City,St. & Zip _____ Gift Rec'd: _____

NAME: _____ Phone: _____

Address: _____

City,St. & Zip _____ Gift Rec'd: _____

NAME: _____ Phone: _____

Address: _____

City,St. & Zip _____ Gift Rec'd: _____

NAME: _____ Phone: _____

Address: _____

City,St. & Zip _____ Gift Rec'd: _____

NAME: _____ Phone: _____

Address: _____

City,St. & Zip _____ Gift Rec'd: _____

NAME: _____ Phone: _____

Address: _____

City,St. & Zip _____ Gift Rec'd: _____

NAME: _____ Phone: _____

Address: _____

City,St. & Zip _____ Gift Rec'd: _____

NAME: _____ Phone: _____

Address: _____

City,St. & Zip _____ Gift Rec'd: _____

BRIDE'S GUEST LIST & GIFTS RECD. CONT.

NAME: _____ Phone: _____

Address: _____

City, St. & Zip _____ Gift Rec'd: _____

NAME: _____ Phone: _____

Address: _____

City, St. & Zip _____ Gift Rec'd: _____

NAME: _____ Phone: _____

Address: _____

City, St. & Zip _____ Gift Rec'd: _____

NAME: _____ Phone: _____

Address: _____

City, St. & Zip _____ Gift Rec'd: _____

NAME: _____ Phone: _____

Address: _____

City, St. & Zip _____ Gift Rec'd: _____

NAME: _____ Phone: _____

Address: _____

City, St. & Zip _____ Gift Rec'd: _____

NAME: _____ Phone: _____

Address: _____

City, St. & Zip _____ Gift Rec'd: _____

NAME: _____ Phone: _____

Address: _____

City, St. & Zip _____ Gift Rec'd: _____

NAME: _____ Phone: _____

Address: _____

City, St. & Zip _____ Gift Rec'd: _____

Groom's Guest List & Gifts Rec'd.

NAME: _____ Phone: _____

Address: _____

City,St. & Zip _____ Gift Rec'd: _____

NAME: _____ Phone: _____

Address: _____

City,St. & Zip _____ Gift Rec'd: _____

NAME: _____ Phone: _____

Address: _____

City,St. & Zip _____ Gift Rec'd: _____

NAME: _____ Phone: _____

Address: _____

City,St. & Zip _____ Gift Rec'd: _____

NAME: _____ Phone: _____

Address: _____

City,St. & Zip _____ Gift Rec'd: _____

NAME: _____ Phone: _____

Address: _____

City,St. & Zip _____ Gift Rec'd: _____

NAME: _____ Phone: _____

Address: _____

City,St. & Zip _____ Gift Rec'd: _____

NAME: _____ Phone: _____

Address: _____

City,St. & Zip _____ Gift Rec'd: _____

NAME: _____ Phone: _____

Address: _____

City,St. & Zip _____ Gift Rec'd: _____

GROOM'S GUEST LIST & GIFTS RECD. CONT.

NAME: _____ Phone: _____

Address: _____

City, St. & Zip _____ Gift Rec'd: _____

NAME: _____ Phone: _____

Address: _____

City, St. & Zip _____ Gift Rec'd: _____

NAME: _____ Phone: _____

Address: _____

City, St. & Zip _____ Gift Rec'd: _____

NAME: _____ Phone: _____

Address: _____

City, St. & Zip _____ Gift Rec'd: _____

NAME: _____ Phone: _____

Address: _____

City, St. & Zip _____ Gift Rec'd: _____

NAME: _____ Phone: _____

Address: _____

City, St. & Zip _____ Gift Rec'd: _____

NAME: _____ Phone: _____

Address: _____

City, St. & Zip _____ Gift Rec'd: _____

NAME: _____ Phone: _____

Address: _____

City, St. & Zip _____ Gift Rec'd: _____

NAME: _____ Phone: _____

Address: _____

City, St. & Zip _____ Gift Rec'd: _____

OUR WEDDING PLANNER GUIDE • 16

GROOM'S GUEST LIST & GIFTS RECD. CONT.

NAME: _____ Phone: _____

Address: _____

City,St. & Zip _____ Gift Rec'd: _____

NAME: _____ Phone: _____

Address: _____

City,St. & Zip _____ Gift Rec'd: _____

NAME: _____ Phone: _____

Address: _____

City,St. & Zip _____ Gift Rec'd: _____

NAME: _____ Phone: _____

Address: _____

City,St. & Zip _____ Gift Rec'd: _____

NAME: _____ Phone: _____

Address: _____

City,St. & Zip _____ Gift Rec'd: _____

NAME: _____ Phone: _____

Address: _____

City,St. & Zip _____ Gift Rec'd: _____

NAME: _____ Phone: _____

Address: _____

City,St. & Zip _____ Gift Rec'd: _____

NAME: _____ Phone: _____

Address: _____

City,St. & Zip _____ Gift Rec'd: _____

NAME: _____ Phone: _____

Address: _____

City,St. & Zip _____ Gift Rec'd: _____

GROOM'S GUEST LIST & GIFTS RECD. CONT.

NAME: _____ Phone: _____

Address: _____

City, St. & Zip _____ Gift Rec'd: _____

NAME: _____ Phone: _____

Address: _____

City, St. & Zip _____ Gift Rec'd: _____

NAME: _____ Phone: _____

Address: _____

City, St. & Zip _____ Gift Rec'd: _____

NAME: _____ Phone: _____

Address: _____

City, St. & Zip _____ Gift Rec'd: _____

NAME: _____ Phone: _____

Address: _____

City, St. & Zip _____ Gift Rec'd: _____

NAME: _____ Phone: _____

Address: _____

City, St. & Zip _____ Gift Rec'd: _____

NAME: _____ Phone: _____

Address: _____

City, St. & Zip _____ Gift Rec'd: _____

NAME: _____ Phone: _____

Address: _____

City, St. & Zip _____ Gift Rec'd: _____

NAME: _____ Phone: _____

Address: _____

City, St. & Zip _____ Gift Rec'd: _____

GROOM'S GUEST LIST & GIFTS RECD. CONT.

NAME: _____ Phone: _____

Address: _____

City,St. & Zip _____ Gift Rec'd: _____

NAME: _____ Phone: _____

Address: _____

City,St. & Zip _____ Gift Rec'd: _____

NAME: _____ Phone: _____

Address: _____

City,St. & Zip _____ Gift Rec'd: _____

NAME: _____ Phone: _____

Address: _____

City,St. & Zip _____ Gift Rec'd: _____

NAME: _____ Phone: _____

Address: _____

City,St. & Zip _____ Gift Rec'd: _____

NAME: _____ Phone: _____

Address: _____

City,St. & Zip _____ Gift Rec'd: _____

NAME: _____ Phone: _____

Address: _____

City,St. & Zip _____ Gift Rec'd: _____

NAME: _____ Phone: _____

Address: _____

City,St. & Zip _____ Gift Rec'd: _____

NAME: _____ Phone: _____

Address: _____

City,St. & Zip _____ Gift Rec'd: _____

GROOM'S GUEST LIST & GIFTS RECD. CONT.

NAME: _____ Phone: _____

Address: _____

City,St. & Zip _____ Gift Rec'd: _____

NAME: _____ Phone: _____

Address: _____

City,St. & Zip _____ Gift Rec'd: _____

NAME: _____ Phone: _____

Address: _____

City,St. & Zip _____ Gift Rec'd: _____

NAME: _____ Phone: _____

Address: _____

City,St. & Zip _____ Gift Rec'd: _____

NAME: _____ Phone: _____

Address: _____

City,St. & Zip _____ Gift Rec'd: _____

NAME: _____ Phone: _____

Address: _____

City,St. & Zip _____ Gift Rec'd: _____

NAME: _____ Phone: _____

Address: _____

City,St. & Zip _____ Gift Rec'd: _____

NAME: _____ Phone: _____

Address: _____

City,St. & Zip _____ Gift Rec'd: _____

NAME: _____ Phone: _____

Address: _____

City,St. & Zip _____ Gift Rec'd: _____

GROOM'S GUEST LIST & GIFTS RECD. CONT.

NAME: _____ Phone: _____

Address: _____

City,St. & Zip _____ Gift Rec'd: _____

NAME: _____ Phone: _____

Address: _____

City,St. & Zip _____ Gift Rec'd: _____

NAME: _____ Phone: _____

Address: _____

City,St. & Zip _____ Gift Rec'd: _____

NAME: _____ Phone: _____

Address: _____

City,St. & Zip _____ Gift Rec'd: _____

NAME: _____ Phone: _____

Address: _____

City,St. & Zip _____ Gift Rec'd: _____

NAME: _____ Phone: _____

Address: _____

City,St. & Zip _____ Gift Rec'd: _____

NAME: _____ Phone: _____

Address: _____

City,St. & Zip _____ Gift Rec'd: _____

NAME: _____ Phone: _____

Address: _____

City,St. & Zip _____ Gift Rec'd: _____

NAME: _____ Phone: _____

Address: _____

City,St. & Zip _____ Gift Rec'd: _____

GROOM'S GUEST LIST & GIFTS RECD. CONT.

NAME: _____ Phone: _____

Address: _____

City,St. & Zip _____ Gift Rec'd: _____

NAME: _____ Phone: _____

Address: _____

City,St. & Zip _____ Gift Rec'd: _____

NAME: _____ Phone: _____

Address: _____

City,St. & Zip _____ Gift Rec'd: _____

NAME: _____ Phone: _____

Address: _____

City,St. & Zip _____ Gift Rec'd: _____

NAME: _____ Phone: _____

Address: _____

City,St. & Zip _____ Gift Rec'd: _____

NAME: _____ Phone: _____

Address: _____

City,St. & Zip _____ Gift Rec'd: _____

NAME: _____ Phone: _____

Address: _____

City,St. & Zip _____ Gift Rec'd: _____

NAME: _____ Phone: _____

Address: _____

City,St. & Zip _____ Gift Rec'd: _____

NAME: _____ Phone: _____

Address: _____

City,St. & Zip _____ Gift Rec'd: _____

GROOM'S GUEST LIST & GIFTS RECD. CONT.

NAME: _____ Phone: _____

Address: _____

City,St. & Zip _____ Gift Rec'd: _____

NAME: _____ Phone: _____

Address: _____

City,St. & Zip _____ Gift Rec'd: _____

NAME: _____ Phone: _____

Address: _____

City,St. & Zip _____ Gift Rec'd: _____

NAME: _____ Phone: _____

Address: _____

City,St. & Zip _____ Gift Rec'd: _____

NAME: _____ Phone: _____

Address: _____

City,St. & Zip _____ Gift Rec'd: _____

NAME: _____ Phone: _____

Address: _____

City,St. & Zip _____ Gift Rec'd: _____

NAME: _____ Phone: _____

Address: _____

City,St. & Zip _____ Gift Rec'd: _____

NAME: _____ Phone: _____

Address: _____

City,St. & Zip _____ Gift Rec'd: _____

NAME: _____ Phone: _____

Address: _____

City,St. & Zip _____ Gift Rec'd: _____

Our Wedding Vows

Bride

_____

_____

_____

_____

_____

_____

_____

_____

_____

_____

_____

_____

_____

Groom

_____

_____

_____

_____

_____

_____

_____

_____

_____

_____

_____

_____

_____

_____

_____

Wedding Ceremony Program

Use this page to outline the order of your service.

Wedding Attire

Bride:

_____
_____
_____
_____

Bridesmaids:

_____
_____
_____
_____

Flower Girl:

_____
_____

Mothers:

_____
_____
_____
_____

Groom:

_____
_____

Groomsmen:

_____
_____

Ring Bearer:

_____
_____

Other:

_____
_____
_____

Bridal Showers

Date

Hostess

Special Memories

_____

_____

_____

_____

_____

_____

_____

_____

_____

Date Thank-you notes sent

Date

Hostess

Special Memories

_____

_____

_____

_____

_____

_____

_____

_____

Date Thank-you notes sent

Bridesmaids' Party

Date

Location

Menu

Thank-you Gifts

Special Memories

Bachelors' Party

Date

Host

Location

Menu

Thank-you Gifts

Special Memories

Rehearsal Dinner Estimates

Date

Location _____ Phone

Address

Menu

Note: _____ Cost per person $

Chosen? ☐ Yes ☐ No

Location _____ Phone

Address

Menu

Note: _____ Cost per person $

Chosen? ☐ Yes ☐ No

Location _____ Phone

Address

Menu

Note: _____ Cost per person $

Chosen? ☐ Yes ☐ No

Wedding Day Transportation

(This form may be photocopied and handed out to those who are responsible for the transportation of the wedding party).

Wedding of _____ Phone _____

Address _____

Wedding Date _____ Time _____

Ceremony and site address _____

_____

Contact person _____ Phone _____

Reception _____ Time _____

Site and address _____

_____

Contact person _____ Phone _____

Type of vehicles _____ Number needed _____

Get me to the church on time:

  Bride _____ Time _____

  Address _____

  _____ Phone _____

  Groom _____ Time _____

  Address _____

  _____ Phone _____

  Parents _____ Time _____

  Address _____

  _____ Phone _____

  Parents _____ Time _____

  Address _____

  _____ Phone _____

WEDDING DAY TRANSPORTATION CONTINUED

Grandparents	Time
Address	
	Phone
Grandparents	Time
Address	
	Phone
Grandparents	Time
Address	
	Phone
Grandparents	Time
Address	
	Phone
Other	Time
Address	
	Phone
Other	Time
Address	
	Phone
Other	Time
Address	
	Phone
Other	Time
Address	
	Phone
Other	Time
Address	
	Phone

Ushers' Duties

Names of ushers

1. Candle lighting:

   _____ & _____

2. Escort in and out...

   the groom's grandmother. Row # _____ , _____

   the bride's grandmother. Row # _____ , _____

   the groom's mother. Row # _____ , _____

   the bride's mother. Row # _____ , _____

3. Special seating:

   Name _____ Row # _____ , _____

   Name _____ Row # _____ , _____

   Name _____ Row # _____ , _____

   Name _____ Row # _____ , _____

   Name _____ Row # _____ , _____

4. Place and remove seating ribbons.

   _____ & _____

5. Place aisle runner.

   _____ & _____

6. Dismiss the wedding guests.

   _____ & _____

7. Removal of flowers to the reception site (when reception is being held at another location).

   _____ & _____

8. Additional Assignments

   _____

   _____

   _____

   _____

   _____

Reception Coordinator

Reception of: _____

Reception site _____ Room _____

Contact person _____ Phone _____

Date _____ Time _____ Planned length _____

Reception Coordinator _____

Phone _____

1. Rooms available for decorating:

   When: _____

   By whom: _____

   Contact person at reception site _____

2. Rental equipment to be delivered or picked up:

   What: _____

   When: _____

   By whom: _____

3. Tables and chairs set up:

   Location: _____

   When: _____

   By whom: _____

4. Cake delivered or picked up:

   When: _____

   By whom: _____

5. Flowers:

   Contact person _____ Phone _____

   Delivered from florist _____

   Flowers transported to reception site _____

   When _____

   By whom _____

RECEPTION COORDINATOR CONTINUED

6. Musicians:

Contact person _____ Phone _____

7. Food and Beverages: _____

Contact person _____ Phone _____

8. "Hostesses":

Guest book _____

Gifts _____

Cake cutting and serving _____

Serving beverages _____

Distributing rice/bird seed _____

9. Clean up and storage:

item: _____

when: _____ by whom: _____

deliver to: _____

Bride's gown _____

left over wedding cake _____

gifts _____

decorations _____

Other _____

_____

_____

_____

_____

_____

_____

_____

Important Phone Numbers

BRIDE _____

Phone: *home* _____ *work* _____

GROOM _____

Phone: *home* _____ *work* _____

MAID OF HONOR _____

Phone: *home* _____ *work* _____

BEST MAN _____

Phone: *home* _____ *work* _____

OFFICIANT _____

Phone: *home* _____ *work* _____

PARENTS

_____ Phone _____

_____ Phone _____

_____ Phone _____

_____ Phone _____

_____ Phone _____

_____ Phone _____

BRIDAL PARTY

_____ Phone _____

_____ Phone _____

_____ Phone _____

_____ Phone _____

_____ Phone _____

_____ Phone _____

_____ Phone _____

_____ Phone _____

_____ Phone _____

_____ Phone _____

_____ Phone _____

IMPORTANT PHONE NUMBERS CONTINUED

	Phone
_____	Phone _____
_____	Phone _____
_____	Phone _____
_____	Phone _____
_____	Phone _____
_____	Phone _____
_____	Phone _____

RING BEARER _____ Phone _____

FLOWER GIRL _____ Phone _____

SOLOISTS

_____ Phone _____

_____ Phone _____

_____ Phone _____

MUSICIANS

_____ Phone _____

_____ Phone _____

_____ Phone _____

PHOTOGRAPHERS/VIDEO/AUDIO

_____ Phone _____

_____ Phone _____

_____ Phone _____

_____ Phone _____

FLORIST

_____ Phone _____

_____ Phone _____

CATERER/BAKERY

_____ Phone _____

_____ Phone _____

IMPORTANT PHONE NUMBERS CONTINUED

RENTAL EQUIPMENT

_____ Phone _____

_____ Phone _____

CEREMONY RECEPTION SITE

_____ Phone _____

_____ Phone _____

_____ Phone _____

PARTY HOSTESSES

_____ Phone _____

_____ Phone _____

_____ Phone _____

_____ Phone _____

OTHERS

_____ Phone _____

_____ Phone _____

_____ Phone _____

_____ Phone _____

_____ Phone _____

_____ Phone _____

_____ Phone _____

_____ Phone _____

_____ Phone _____

_____ Phone _____

_____ Phone _____

_____ Phone _____

_____ Phone _____

_____ Phone _____

_____ Phone _____

_____ Phone _____